Other books by Mary Summer Rain

NONFICTION

Spirit Song*

Phoenix Rising*

Dreamwalker*

Phantoms Afoot*

Earthway

Daybreak

Soul Sounds

Whispered Wisdom

Ancient Echoes

Bittersweet

Mary Summer Rain's Guide
to Dream Symbols

The Visitation*

Millennium Memories

Fireside

Eclipse

The Singing Web

Beyond Earthway

Trined in Twilight

Pinecones

Love Never Sleeps

CHILDREN'S

Mountains, Meadows, and Moonbeams

Star Babies

FICTION

The Seventh Mesa

*ALSO SOLD AS AUDIOBOOKS

Mary Summer Rain

earthway's wisdom for daily living from grandmother earth

TAO OF NATURE

a fireside book PUBLISHED BY SIMON & SCHUSTER
NEW YORK LONDON TORONTO SYDNEY SINGAPORE

FIRESIDE
Rockefeller Center
1230 Avenue of the Americas
New York, NY 10020

For information regarding special discounts for bulk purchases,
please contact Simon & Schuster Special Sales:
1-800-456-6798 or business@simonandschuster.com

DESIGNED BY ELINA D. NUDELMAN

Manufactured in the United States of America

10 9 8 7 6 5 4 3 2 1

Library of Congress Cataloging-in-Publication Data

Summer Rain, Mary, 1945–
The tao of nature: earthway's wisdom for daily living from Grandmother Earth / Mary Summer Rain.
p.cm.
1. Spiritual life. 2. Nature–Religious aspects. I. Title.

BL435 .S86 2002
291.2'12–dc21 2002021178

ISBN 0-7434-0790-3

TO THE MOST PROFOUND PHILOSOPHER OF ALL TIME,
TO THE WISEST TEACHER EVER,
WHO EMBODIES THE SWEET AND GENTLE TAO OF NATURE—
THE OLD WOMAN OF THE WOODS.
TO HER I FONDLY AND MOST GRATEFULLY DEDICATE THIS BOOK.

contents

foreword
nature, reality—the two terms being truly synonymous

NATURE. TEACHER. BOTH TERMS BEING INTERchangeable.

Grandmother Earth, the wise Old Woman of the Woods, the greatest Teacher of all. At every turn Her wisdom is freely gifted to us in generous offerings of love–offerings of Herself–regardless of whether we have the clear eyes to see, the open ears to hear, the knowing minds to perceive, or the sensitive hearts to receive. So often humans ignore Her spectacular attributes and generous bounties and, when they do recognize them, often rip out Her riches without thought or a respectful thanksgiving for what they've received. People don't usually count Her treasured gifts as blessings but see them as possessions they believe they've every "right" to claim as their own.

They argue over those rights. They become aggressive and even resort to violence in order to gain possession of them.

Nature is an entity unto itself. No part of it belongs to a single human upon this magnificent planet. Nature belongs to the Creatrix who breathed life into all God physically manifested in the Beginning. This is what our perspective of Nature should be. Grandmother Earth is the Old Woman of the Woods who holds the Wellspring of Sacred Knowledge for right living, which She continually displays for us to perceive, learn, and grow from, through Her lessons in Nature. These jewels of wisdom are indeed invaluable assets to us. They are crystal clear gems offered to our receiving minds. We should acknowledge and accept them with gratitude. We cannot afford to remain blind to these ancient and timeless philosophical gifts and the greater value they carry within the external wrappings of flora and fauna. There are many lessons to be gleaned–and learned–from that which lies within nature's physical beauty. And so do we need to peer beyond the awesome sunsets and beneath the splendorous blanket of meadow wildflowers to the Within of them, where the true gifts–the lessons–lie hidden, just waiting for our minds to unwrap them and revel in their wisdom.

The Old Woman of the Woods, with the shimmering divine spirit of the Grand Dame Creatrix glowing vibrantly within Her tender breast, is everywhere. Her wisdom abounds in all facets of Nature, from the sun-drenched desert dunes to the shimmering alpine snowfield, She is there. She is there waiting for us, not to greedily take but to gently recognize with our minds and to respectfully receive with our hearts what She offers us moment by moment, day by day.

In these pages I offer up some of the thoughts, reflections, and lessons I have gathered from the natural world around me. I hope my insights and observations of the wisdom of the Old Woman of the Woods help you see Her presence more clearly, more often in your own life. Open your senses, your heart, and your soul to Her timeless teachings.

TAO OF NATURE

mariposa morning—beauty of beingness

ON ONE FRAGRANTLY WARM AND SUNNY spring morn, I awoke to the cheery birdsong of dawn and found that my entire being was bursting with excitement over the bright new day. Budding life whispered to me from the fertile earth and the alpine air that was as sweet as sugared strawberries. My yearning spirit desperately wanted to sample these special offerings of spring in the mountains more directly. Happy to satisfy the gnawing hunger I felt growing within me, I quietly snuck out of my cabin and headed straight for the newly greened forest.

Birdsong chirped and trilled all about me.

High in a towering blue spruce, the resident crow cawed her routine greeting. Being neighborly, I immediately responded in kind and talked to her for some time. Cocking her glistening head this way and that, the crow curiously looked down at me and chortled back. How wonderful it'd be, I thought, if all the different species of life could truly understand one another through a single common language and actually converse. Ah, well.

Sunrays silently undulated down through the high pines, casting sprinkles of glittering light on leaves and pine needles. As the sun climbed, this molten gold spread in ever-widening tide pools over the forest floor. This ground beneath my feet was a carpet of rebirthing life. Infant leaves of all shapes and sizes, swaddled in many shades of newborn green, were reaching and stretching toward the nourishing brightness.

The awe of all this wonderful budding life, so precious and fragile, yet so incredibly tenacious, filled my senses. At this elevation of nearly 10,000 feet where I live in the Colorado Rockies, the pussy willow–like aspen buds had dropped away to reveal emerging leaves, bringing the delight of a new green tint throughout the woodlands. I'd waited with eager anticipation to see this happen, as my mountain elevation causes all of nature to trail a month or more behind its siblings in the cities and towns down below.

Whenever I'd have occasion to journey to Colorado Springs to do errands in May, the city's nature would already be wearing deep green garb and flowering trees would be dressed in a profusion of blossoms, while the nature surrounding my cabin high up on the mountain would still be in winter white. Seeing this great disparity always brought about in me a great eagerness for my neighboring woods to catch up. So now, when the first of June showed its face and the trees around my cabin finally showed signs of rubbing the long winter's nap from their sleepy eyes, I too felt an exploding sense of rebirth and felt magnetically drawn to the new life that was birthing all around me. This is how I came to be in the forest on such a warm and bright early June morn. My woods had finally awakened.

I had no worn footpaths through these forests, for my journeys through them would always follow the wanderlust of my free spirit. This particular morn was no different as I carefully picked my way through the dense new growth of golden pea, wild strawberries, white fleabane, and lavender asters. I had no preplanned destination in mind. Instead I focused on merely enjoying all that I saw and felt within nature's pure essence.

Wafting up from the earth was a fertile fragrance that brought strong impressions of a verdant life force, which I likened to the Earth Mother's umbilical, throbbing with enough nutrients to sustain all of nature's thirsting needs. And the scent, the scent was her womanly fragrance of pungent fertility.

As the warming sunlight pranced atop the tender greenery around my feet, I felt as though I'd been drawn into its merriment while it also tiptoed with the touch of fairy feet over my head and across my shoulders.

The light breath of breeze gently rustled the baby aspen leaves and hushed a soothing lullaby that blended with the cheery birdsong. Such magical music brought out in me a heart smile that surely would be shared by all who heard it.

The dancing.

The scents.

The chiming music of nature.

Nature dancing and hypnotically swaying to its own lilting rhythm of life, its own fragile, yet eternally strong, drumming heartbeat. The heartbeat giving evidence of the tender metered pulse of the Old Woman of the Woods's eternal, living presence. Her sacred Presence was all about me. Her life force provided the beat of nature's sweet song, for truly I knew that walking into these living woods was the same as walking through the very soul of Her. Therefore, I placed each of my footsteps ever so softly and attentively lest I unintentionally cause Her pain or disrupt the soft and soothing rhythm of Her pulse.

Carefully I moved deeper and deeper into the woodlands while my hungry soul began satiating itself with the sensual natural offerings. Now that this high country earth had become provocatively warm and fertile once again, there was so much to look at, so many new wonders to notice and take in that my senses verged on overload.

Tingling with sensory fulfillment, I forced myself to pause and catch my breath. I held the moment suspended.

I closed my eyes.

And slowly exhaled.

When I opened them again, something stark white in the distant greenery caught my eye. I had the sense that I was no longer alone, that some dynamic Presence had joined me, that the Old Woman of the Woods had silently sidled up beside me, pointing Her golden finger at something She wished me to go look at.

Granting Her wish, I cautiously wove my way through the infant undergrowth. And to my amazement, when nearing the sunlit whiteness, I saw a lone mariposa lily in full bloom. It was far too early in the season for these mountain wildflowers to appear; they normally don't blanket the hillsides and forest floors until July. What a wonder this was. What a discovery it was to come upon this solitary lily standing so beautiful and apart from the rest of the newly sprouting carpet of thriving greenery.

Without daring to touch the fragile blossom, I glanced about for a proper place to sit without disturbing any growing things. I wanted to just sit and look at the fantastic discovery and think about the unexpected presence of this small but majestic woodland wonder.

Its stem was tall and strong.

The blossom, white as new-fallen snow on Christmas Eve.

Within the petals' sweet depths, the deep maroon lining was rich and called to mind the velvety, royal purple robes of Camelot's Queen Guinevere. The word *stately* quickly came to mind. This lone lily was stately. It was stately in its own natural beingness. Indeed, its pure beauty needed no admiration of mine or anyone else's to give it purpose or reason to exist.

So too is the inner beauty of every single individual. Every person on this planet has an incredible uniqueness that is her or his own singular imprint, a characteristic exclusiveness that shines forth from the core beingness and is as strikingly beautiful and distinctive as that pristine mariposa lily standing apart from all other life-forms growing in those deep woods.

That lily is us.

We are that lily.

Yet few realize that this is so, for they believe they need the admiration or approval of others in order to feel personal worth–to be as outstanding as that white lily among all the greenery surrounding it. They feel they need to "be somebody" in life or to have a grandiose personal "purpose." This is because they don't recognize the splendor of their inner beingness, which makes them stand out without another's notice or admiration.

Society has formed an ironclad ideology of greatness and worth–of what makes people special or outstanding. Society has voluntarily put on the blinders so it doesn't recognize everyone's uniqueness and magnificent individuality. As our society has become focused on celebrity-sized greatness, each person appears to have adopted a diminutive perception of the Self. This is so evident in the letters I receive from readers who believe one's "purpose in life" needs to be nothing less than a great, publicly recognized accomplishment in order to be worthwhile. They feel they must become renowned teachers, celebrated healers, or popular psychics. I can't count the number of times I've advised people to not define their goal in life as the accomplishment of *one* thing but rather make their *entire* lives an accomplishment.

A fulfilling life is guided by acts of continual unconditional goodness. It is an accomplishment that is attained on a daily and hourly basis throughout one's entire life. This way of living is the epitome of greatness and the path on which we recognize our own self-worth. Yet, on the whole, folks just don't understand the concepts of accomplishment and greatness as those attributes are associated with self-worth. Therefore, many people never enjoy the satisfaction of perceiving the beauty of basic beingness within themselves and others. Nobody thinks she's anybody unless she's Somebody–never realizing that *everyone* is a Somebody . . . a very unique Somebody.

We all have these beautiful qualities that make us peerless in our own right. Yes, each one of us is peerless because nobody else is a precise replica of ourselves. Yet I see many who desperately try to replicate the characteristics and accomplishments of others and waste entire lifetimes striving to reach that unattainable goal. People tend to feel they're nobody unless others give them some type of acclaim or recognition. That's pure ego. That's thinking that greatness or self-worth is not achieved unless one's ego gets stroked and stroked again. That's ignoring the beauty within oneself–that natural and inherent beauty of the spirit–that is always there, always waiting to shine forth. To recognize this truth is to reap its benefits. We alone can tap into our greatness. No audience is required.

The Divine sees each individual as a brilliantly shining Light Within. That alone automatically makes everyone a Somebody. Now add to that Light the words and works of Unconditional Goodness and you have a truly great individual who is worth his or her weight in pure gold. Self-Worth is not contingent on peer recognition. It is not born of amassed awards, wealth, or acclaim. Self-Worth is the inner knowing that one is doing good in the world whether it's recognized in a public manner or not. Self-Worth is directly associated with one's inner Beauty of Beingness and how that powerful Beingness positively affects others. No one has to be outwardly recognized in order to feel that wonderful fullness of heart and spirit that a job was well done or that it was a good thing to give another some comfort or compassion. Every time somebody fills a task with the focus of her or his complete being or helps another person in life, that somebody is a spiritual Somebody, and the material awards or recognition for such deeds do not give the act any more spiritual credence than it already had. And they certainly shouldn't make the experience any more meaningful or fulfilling for the one who performed it.

Spiritually speaking, the wealthy and internationally famous film mogul may be no greater or have achieved no more in life than the maid who cleans his mansion or the gardener who maintains his gardens. The maid and gardener may, in fact, feel more self-worth than the mogul just by knowing they're performing their daily jobs well and conscientiously. Every job well done is an achievement, an accomplishment. Every job well done should give one a sense of worth, of being a useful and productive person–an asset. This is because every individual is Somebody to begin with. Every individual is a shimmering Light that can shine out into the world or can be hidden from view. The difference between the two comes down to one's personal choice of how she or he *perceives* that glorious Inner Light. People can understand that their Inner Light of Beingness is shining all the time or they can falsely believe that their Light can only shine and become brighter if others perceive it and admire it. Like the lone mariposa lily out in the deep woods, whose beautiful Light of Beingness radiates day and night, the unique spirit of each of us exists and emanates from within, never needing any external recognition or outside admiration to validate its presence, its radiance.

It just is.

old bristlecone—perseverance

WHENEVER THE NECESSITY CALLS AND I LEAVE MY cabin and travel down to Woodland Park or Colorado Springs for errands or an appointment, I'm presented with the fortunate choice of several routes.

All are twisting and breathtakingly scenic.

All are byways that descend over one thousand feet from my secluded dwelling.

The more popular roads smoothly snake around the mountainsides and precariously slither beside sheer, unguarded drop-offs like a drunken sidewinder. The narrow, two-lane highways see over 90 percent more traffic from locals who, feeling this is their lucky day and having daydreams of winning the big jackpot, are heading up to Cripple

Creek for hours of gambling. These traveling locals are accompanied by throngs of excited tourists piloting all manner of recreational vehicles as they make their hair-raising ascent to take photographs of the historic high-mountain gold-mining town.

The little-used, dusty back roads are frequently reminiscent of my great-grandma's galvanized washboard. They too snake down to the lower elevation yet do not hug the mountainsides as do the alternate roads but rather descend through high canyonlike corridors of rocky cliffs and verdant valleys that open up the vista like a crack in time.

Always. Always, I choose to drive slowly along one back road in particular because that's where the magnificent red-tailed hawks and prairie falcons spread their wings to leisurely cruise the shifting alpine currents like living hang gliders. Along this road is where they perch on the swaying tops of tall jack pines in the afternoon light to warm their speckled breasts and scan the heath below for unwary prey. Along this quiet way to town a family of bighorn sheep can often be spied taking an afternoon stroll over high rock outcroppings and the big-eared mule deer mosey across it or stand along its shoulder to lock their large, shining eyes on yours. Here you can spot an occasional owl rotating her feathery neck as she silently watches you pass beneath her. And the pines that remind me of bristlecones grow along the edge of one of the greater switchbacks of this dusty dirt road.

Bristlecones.

Bristlecone pines.

Beyond the precarious edge of the ridgeline the land gracefully sweeps down into a valley, leaving these trees' ancient bones exposed to winter's updrafts and summer's long hours of intense high-altitude sun. Though the ravages of time and unforgiving weather give the skin of their branches ice burns and sun scorch, the pines' gnarled arms continue to grow undaunted. They extend further into the world each new spring; their branches' twisted extensions are proof of powerful souls pulsing steady and true within their strong heartwood.

And so it is that I am blessed to see the persistence of life, a facet of the Old Woman of the Woods's personality. The beauty of these pines is spectacular not only to the naked eye but also to the eye of the mind, which can take in the wisdom of their continuing will to live and grow.

This is why I choose this dusty, bumpy road whenever necessity beckons me to journey down from my mountain cabin into civilization's little towns and big, bustling cities. Though I admit that I don't always stop at the hairpin switchback and pull off the shoulder to spend time with the special pines I pass, I do find that their inherent character is strong enough to elicit philosophical thoughts about them as I drive by. The sight of them seems to always turn up the corners of my mouth in a slight smile as I am reminded of their inner strength. And the word *perseverance* forever comes to mind. Not only Inner Strength–a strong constitution–but true Perseverance, for that is the *enduring* attribute of the bristlecone's deepest innermost nature.

Aged, yet still growing strong.

Enduring in the face of bitter and searing exposure to unexpected adversity.

Heads never bent in defeat but constantly held high to the light.

A life force forever growing forward with acceptance heavily ingrained in every cellular fiber of the stout heartwood.

Fiber. The bristlecone is made of tenacious interwoven fibers, and those of us who see beyond the surface physicality of life–those who see with their whole perceptual being–also see that the bristlecone pine is the quintessential example of fortitude, the epitome of unrelenting perseverance. And for this alone I see not the twisted and bent limbs but rather the indomitable life force Within that grasps on to life with a knuckle-white hold and says, "I will not let myself be beaten down. I will survive! I am a survivor!"

I am a survivor.

Rarely do I find myself driving past those pines without those words coming to mind, and they naturally lead to thoughts of people who give up so easily and sink into despair, who allow themselves to be bent and crippled by life's bitter winds and emotional pain. People don't realize that they possess the very same inner strength to persevere as the bristlecones do; because of negating and self-defeating thoughts, such as self-pity or need for attention, which weaken that resolve, they allow themselves to feel broken, unable to grow forth into the light of tomorrow's beautiful dawn, or even acknowledge the bright, new possibilities that the next hour or minute may present as healing opportunities.

Perseverance can fill one's beingness so fully that there is not an inch of space left over for self-destructive attitudes such as negativity, self-pity, or moribund thoughts that pull blackness into an individual's perception of self. Perseverance leaves no place for these to hide. It's a choice, a *voluntary* choice. That's what perseverance is. It's a choice that takes a simple shift in perspective. We can focus our view of life inward, wallow in the muck of self-absorbed woe, or we can turn our view outward to a wide-angle shot of the vast world around us, away from the all-consuming I. This is the choice everyone is free to make for himself or herself. But many don't choose to look outward and persevere, because they've somehow gotten it into their heads that such a view requires energy. They feel that they just do not have the strength to look outside themselves when it's so much easier simply to sit in an easy chair, stare at the floor, feel sorry for themselves, and sigh, "Woe is me." Or it's easier to complain to family and friends in an effort to get sympathetic attention and ego-stroking comfort.

When focus is rotated away from ourselves or away from a difficult recent personal event and aimed out into the world, perseverance has the potential to serve as a positive dynamic force in our lives. It can become a powerful attribute that we don't even think about. Looking beyond ourselves, we can face the soft light of the next breaking day, the promise of the next hour and minute, instead of those darker ones that have passed and cannot be altered or in any way erased from our reality. We can gather strength from the small, beautiful moments and events that unfold around us if we just look up and out. If we have this broad view, we can usually find the energy and inspiration to persevere.

It's not easier to wallow in one's woes than to move past them. It's not easier because one has to apply a lot of thought energy–a lot–to those woes to stay trapped in them. By contrast, perseverance is accomplished through the *non-thought* of acceptance when one stands up from that listless "couch slouch" position, shakes off the shards of self-pity and, with firm conviction, says, "Hell with it! What's done is done and I have a life to live!" That's accepting what's "done-an'-done" as just that–done, finished, over with. That's making the choice not to allow yourself to be brought down. That's recognizing that the past is the past and, by God, you're going to stand tall and grab life by its shirttail. You're going to take advantage of and appreciate every beautiful blessing and silver-lined opportunity that it leads you to. That's making the voluntary choice to persevere. That's taking charge of your life instead of letting life take charge of you. That's standing up instead of lying down.

I'm not so idealistic as to believe that people can't be

knocked down; not just once but again and again, until they feel like veritable punching bags. Good grief, no one knows that better than I do. Yet getting knocked down doesn't mean that you have to stay down for the full count. Nope, it doesn't mean that at all. Your heart gets seared by someone's cruel words, or perhaps bitter emotional winds chill your bones with grief or shatter a relationship, or maybe financial problems hail down on you so hard and fast that you can't see any way to get out from under them. Everyone, at one point or another in life, experiences temporary bouts of depression and can be overcome with stressors that make events feel like the world has closed in–like there's no use in going on. But those thoughts are only the immediate knee-jerk reactions to an unexpected tragedy or tribulation.

We humans are made of strong fiber, a resilient fiber that weaves its durable threads through every cell of our beingness. We're survivors, you and I. We're survivors who can rise above the blindsiding blows and tribulations that slap us in the face. Yet this innately beautiful and precious ability of ours to survive can't be known or even felt if we choose to be emotionally "down," stuck fast in a mire of self-deprecation, or to wallow in the consuming woe of self-absorption. When we choose to wrap these self-deceptive and dark perspectives around us, we cannot see past the smothering, defeating fabric of our own making or breathe the fresh air of upcoming positive probabilities. Nor can we even hope to imagine what spectacular possibilities lie on our golden horizon.

Knowing you're made of greater stuff is the first step in not letting yourself stay down for the final count. Realizing that your tomorrows *can* become your today, full of fresh air and sunlight, is the foundation of perseverance. No matter what you face, you always have the choice to welcome this powerful perspective within yourself and fully utilize it.

It's a fact that life can be hard. It's a fact that everyone experiences disappointments and griefs. It's a fact that we all get knocked down. It's not a fact that we have to remain down. So you get knocked down and find yourself looking at the ground. Okay, now you're down. Here's where your opportunity for choice enters in. What are you going to do? Stay down? No way! You move slowly–in steps. First you raise yourself onto your knees while you catch your breath, then you get up on your feet and release a much-needed sigh. You glance around. You look over the damage that's scattered at your feet. You pick up the fragments that can be salvaged. Then you take those pieces–those precious, precious pieces, those glimmering jewels of wisdom–and use them in a constructive *new* manner. With a firm resolve and renewed determination, you continue living and growing. Renewing. Rebuilding. That's perseverance. That's perseverance gained from learning treasured lessons, mining gems of wisdom from life experiences. That's perseverance gleaned from understanding that the buffeting emotional winds and the biting chill of someone's harsh personality, or other storms from the erratic weather of life, cannot keep you pinned down. Those storms are made of illusionary matter, and that's the crux of the whole issue. I repeat, *those storms are illusionary.* Perseverance sees those storms as vaporous images of the mind, while self-pity perceives them as real black clouds that never clear.

Like the century-old bristlecones, we are not left unaffected by all those unexpected bitter chills or searing pains we're exposed to in life, rather we are made more durable for having experienced their touch. We're left with scars that do not vanish from the skin's surface yet have, through time, healed over. Those scars represent learning experiences. Those scars can be either marks of wisdom gained or signs of defeat. You have the choice in defining them. Every bitter wind that buffeted us, every single tear shed, every hurt felt, and every frigid word that froze or sorrowed our hearts is a marker that has served to build a stronger character . . . but only if we choose to see them with the perception of wisdom. And it's this choice to learn and grow from life's difficult challenges that strengthens the flow of perseverance through the heartwood of one's fiber.

Life may bend our backs a bit. Life may slap us in the face and leave our cheeks stinging, it may even land us on the ground with some hard, well-aimed blows. Life may leave scars upon our hearts and trip us so that we stumble and fall. But we're made of greater stuff–we have spirit. We have an intellectual choice and we have the precious gift of wisdom. We can choose either to continually moan and wince as we scratch at and open wounds of the past or to acknowledge those wounds with acceptance in our hearts and, with perseverance burning like a roaring fire in our souls, turn our faces to the golden potential of a sunlit tomorrow and, while walking into that warm and inviting light called Our Future, shout, "I'm a survivor!"

The old bristlecone . . . a survivor. A survivor by nature.

The human constitution . . . a survivor. A survivor by choice.

her royal highness—growing into wisdom

I LIVED IN THE ROCKY MOUNTAINS OF COLORADO for twenty-two years before I was able to have a real flower garden. By a flower garden I mean one that is big enough to stroll through, not merely flowers in a few pots on the front stoop, or herbs growing in the kitchen windowsill, or houseplants on a desktop. I always wanted one, I just never lived in a place long enough to plant a real outside garden and have the surety that I'd be there the following summer to enjoy it. Though I'd find myself filling out and sending in all those tear-out forms for the usual seed and bulb catalogs year after year, I never placed an order after the magazines came. I couldn't bear to plant bulbs in the fall when I might not be there the following season to see their green fingertips push aside the melting spring snow so their colorful heads could poke through.

I love flowers. I absolutely love them. Always have. And I'd daydream of living in a Cotswold cottage cosseted beneath flowering vines. Lush greenery full of flowers. This dream cottage would have no boring green lawn but rather a yard full of colorful blossoms. Ahh, those daydreams kept me going as I conjured up visions of a "someday place" while looking through all those nursery catalogs. I was optimistic that one day I'd finally be able to place an order from those pages of blossoms. For twenty-two years I said, "Maybe next year," never losing faith that that "next year" would indeed arrive.

When the nineteenth year rolled around, 1996 had arrived, and I found myself in a very special, very magical place that, for the first time, gave off no sense of impermanence, had no hint of being a temporary dwelling. This magical place was an unfinished cedar cabin that drew its electric power from a retired hospital generator. It was surrounded by aspen and conifer woods and overlooked a serene mountain valley. Our closest neighbor was a city-dwelling family who visited their rustic cabin only a couple of times a year during the summer months. Their place was perched atop a ridge across the valley.

When I first stood on the weathered planks of the cabin's covered front porch and let my hungry eyes scan the delicious valley, I felt my soul sample the sweetness of the far mountain peaks beyond it and my spirit welled with deep joy and peacefulness. *Ohh, this is the place,* I remember thinking. *This is the place I could die in!*

On the surface, this last thought doesn't exactly appear to be one that would bring visuals of complete happiness to mind, yet that's just what it did for me. I had finally found a place to rest my weary bones and, in complete contentedness and tranquillity, live out the rest of my days. I felt I'd finally reached that formerly elusive place called Home. Together with my friend Sally, I met with my attorney to form a legal "partnership to purchase real estate" and bought it.

Because the cabin was unfinished, we had many work projects that took priority over a flower garden. Indeed, when we first arrived a flower garden seemed frivolous compared with the more pressing work to be done. Yet the surety of it becoming reality was always in my mind. It simmered like a slow-cooking ham bone soup on the back burner. In the summer of 1999, after we'd worked for three years on the cabin, the time finally came for the flower garden to go in. I couldn't contain my excitement, and my energy spiked and sparked in all directions. I felt like a little kid. My Child Within was laughing and skipping around with the joy of attaining a long-held dream.

Our first task in creating the flower bed was digging out a massive sloped bank to improve drainage beside the cabin foundation. Then we got down on hands and knees with shovels and trowels to carve out steps and install heavy railroad ties. We made the stairs and two retaining walls. Next we terraced the garden area itself. Last we added the many white quartz rocks we'd collected on hikes to create a rock garden. Then the glorious day of days came when Sally returned from errands in town to surprise me with armloads of flats filled with all types of flowers.

Flats of giggling pansy faces for the window boxes.

Flats of deep purple petunias for around the birdbaths.

Flats and flats of bright yellow and brilliant red perennials.

She brought those plants that would grow tall along the fence line and those that would quickly spread around their feet and cover the ground. In the back of the old pickup she had more–two lilac trees and three clematis vines! I squealed and raced to the potting shed she'd built for me the summer before. I happily exited it. Ta–da! Ceremoniously I held the two trowels aloft as though they were golden nuggets we'd panned from one of our sparkling valley streams. It didn't matter at all to me what kinds of flowers she'd brought because I loved them all. I loved every sweet petal.

Eventually we got all the plants' delicate feet firmly planted in their new homes and, for the following few weeks, I mothered them like newborn babies through high–mountain hail, sudden thunder snowstorms, and tree–bending winds. Every single flower, every one–from the blooming clematis and foxglove to the tiny soapworts, chiming bells, and Johnny–jump–ups–made it through to feel the touch of the sweet, warmer days of summer on their smiling faces. I couldn't have been happier. At least that's what I thought at the time.

I thought I couldn't be happier until all of the flowers' fragrant petals drew the fragile winged beings who flitted and danced about the brilliantly colored blossoms. It seemed that, overnight, dozens of butterflies appeared as if by the magical sweep of the Fairy Queen's sparkling wand. Or perhaps the Old Woman of the Woods Herself had decided that the new garden lacked some additional living element of Her special touch. Whatever the cause, I delighted in the fluttering activity and spent hours just sitting on the garden bench watching the incredible fragility of the butterflies. I would like to think they felt my admiration.

It was on one of these spectacularly sunny alpine days of summer when I sat on the garden bench that I was gifted with a visit by the Mother of them all–a magnificent Monarch. Her Highness had come to grace the new garden with her royal presence. Perhaps she'd come to see what all the fuss was about. Perhaps Her Ladyship had come with gossamer glints of wing dust to leave behind her seal of acceptance. Or perhaps she'd merely come to sup from the cups of Mother Nature's intoxicating new nectars that'd suddenly sprouted up from this formerly barren ground. It really wasn't important to me what the reason for her appearance was because I was just plain tickled to see her come every day and flutter from petal to velvet petal like a prima ballerina who knows the world's her stage and each flower blossom a separate colored footlight shining on her alone.

The more I watched this magnificently winged wonder of nature, the more my thoughts of her were associated with wisdom. How splendorous she was in her beauty. How light and airy was her character. Focused, yet never blinded to the world around her, she exhibited signs of peripheral awareness. She was not aloof but rather visibly acknowledged all other dusty-winged species that she encountered without exhibiting any sign of expecting or demanding deference. I noticed that this Queen was a bit of a loner as she went about her business.

Butterflies.

The grand Monarch.

Wings, made so translucent and fragile-looking, were backlit by the brilliance of the afternoon sun. Wings as colorful as stained glass. Wing fabric so fine as to be unattainable by even kings and queens. Fabric that cannot be bought at any price. Fabric obtained only through a metamorphosis from within. Butterflies, the transformed core of beingness. And the resplendent beauties and blessings of wisdom come to kiss this new garden with sweet touches of living vibrant color and silent murmurings. Messages only the acutely observant mind and still, quiet soul can hear.

From whence comes this magnificent embodiment of wisdom?

What high magic has been wrought by some adept Sorceress of Light to make it appear?

What enchanted forest does it call home?

Silly questions all. As silly as people searching high and low for wisdom. As silly as folks thinking wisdom is the same thing as knowledge or equating it to intelligence, for though people can spend a lifetime reading and learning, though they be born with a Mensa-level intelligence quotient, wisdom will not be theirs until it has slowly and with gentleness grown quietly forth from deep within themselves. Some mystical sorceress didn't weave a spell to materialize those radiant wings of wisdom. There is no enchanted forest where wisdom resides. And an elegant cape of it can't be bought on Rodeo Drive.

Wisdom is not an attribute that can be gained overnight. It's not something one can be seeking on Wednesday and suddenly find on Thursday afternoon. It's not a buried treasure discovered by a metal detector, it's not hidden in a chest among gold doubloons in a sunken ship. Wisdom can't be bought and it can't be found. It can't be gifted or stolen away. Wisdom can only come from within the self through a slow transformation process that involves the intellect, common sense, and acceptance. And so this process of transformation is likened to that of the beautiful butterfly's timely metamorphosis. It begins with the crawling caterpillar.

A caterpillar. A slow-moving life force anchored to the ground, the touchable surface of life. A being imprisoned in the physicality of its own limited reality. Its entire perception is derived only through that which it can touch, that which it can firmly set its feet upon. Its knowable scope of reality–its worldview–is restricted to what it sees in front of its face. Its daily perception of life is a microscopic one, never affording it the ability to peer into or even imagine a more telescopic view of its world.

Most people are much like that caterpillar. They're convinced that they can only believe in that which they can touch or see. Their perception is imprisoned. Perception is confined to a self-created ground on which they surround themselves with only the tactile elements of their world. Imagination is firmly tethered to that ground. Dreams and goals are securely held down to it, never allowed to fly aloft and experience a panoramic eagle's-eye view of reality. Creativity is self-limiting. Possibilities are nonexistent.

Here is where folks think that knowledge, advanced schooling, intelligence, and cleverness are synonymous with wisdom. Here is where people have the idea that personal talents, skills, and psychic abilities are end-all goals or the pinnacle of their lives' strivings. Here is where they stop and pat themselves on the back, believing that their goals have been reached and their ideologies are spotlessly perfected. They're as proud of their individual accomplishments as a cooking school student is proud of her first soufflé. Except . . . except when it comes to the truth of their situation–they forgot to put it into the oven.

Schooling, intelligence, knowledge, or special talents can *enhance* wisdom. But they are not wisdom. They aren't even necessary elements of it. Now is that idea a shocker, or what? It will be to those who are keeping their perspectives tethered to the tactile aspects of life. They will always be the perceptual caterpillars of the world. Those who believe they are wise and wonderful just because they have some knowledge, intelligence, or a bit of skill. But those caterpillars who wonder, those who have some inner sense and yearning that there's something more than the ground they place their feet upon, those who are open to possibilities are the ones who welcome the idea of exploring such dreams further. They are the ones who dare to contemplate the possibilities and have the vision to see how far-reaching they could be.

They look around at the touchable place they're in and

ponder their visions. They boldly begin to speculate on other realms and one day find that they're no longer satisfied with those former limiting beliefs and realize that . . . there's so much more. One day they pull into themselves to think about all the knowns and discover how limited they are. On this day they find that they're no longer satisfied, that they need to think more deeply on things, that they have to contemplate life and their narrow view of it. On this day the true scope of living reality dawns on them and they're compelled to delve into it with their whole beingness. On this day Thought becomes their Cocoon, and they become the Chrysalis.

And so it is that those who no longer equate intelligence or talent with wisdom realize that they are not the end-all products of perfection but rather developing pupae within the hard shell of possibilities. The shell, composed of a tight silken weave of endless ideas, potentialities, philosophies, and subtle inner knowings, surrounds the mind of the chrysalislike human with the transforming energies of an ever-widening perspective. Time passes. Time passes while we absorb That Which Is. Time passes while we slowly come to greater understandings about life and contemplate the meanings of new epiphanies. Time passes while we grow greater with renewed Cells of Wisdom that bring about the metamorphosis from a base and limited mind-set into the beautiful spiritually advanced human beings we were meant to be.

For some, the chrysalis stage is long. For some, it's short. For others, it never comes at all. But those for whom it does come emerge with a beautiful life perspective full of the joy that wisdom has instilled. These visionaries rise above the others of their former kind who, through their own choosing, still cling to their touchable, ground perspectives while crawling through their limited reality. And when the new butterfly spreads its powdery wings for the first time, it lifts itself away from the cocoon. Away. Away! Spreading wings wide, it revels in the lightness of its body and rejoices in the airy freedom the Knowing of Wisdom has brought. Looking down, it inherently accepts its cousins on the ground with the understanding that they're where they're content. The butterfly feels no sadness because it knows that they're where they choose to be. It knows that their vision does not extend to Possibilities. And with this thought, the butterfly flits off to share what it has learned, spreading golden pollen of wisdom from one receiving petal to the next.

People. Some being caterpillars, never knowing what wisdom is. Some encased in a chrysalis, just discovering that Possibility surrounds them and . . . being in the process of growing into it. Others are butterflies going silently about, sharing the wisdom they have through simple example and beautiful works.

These were the thoughts that came to me as I sat on my garden bench and watched the monarch touch each blossom heart.

Her Royal Highness–a living example of the spectacular beauty and freedom of Wisdom. Wisdom that exists in and of itself, demanding or expecting nothing. Quiet Wisdom. Solid and true. Wisdom soft . . . soft as butterfly wings.

eye of the falcon — recognizing blessings

ON ONE PARTICULARLY BEAUTIFUL AND BRILliantly sunny afternoon in late summer while my companion was in town attending to errands, I was home having one hell of a time trying to work on a book. Creativity remained elusive, forcing me to play a catch-me-if-you-can game with it. The deep blue sky beckoning from the window behind my computer monitor was not making it any easier for me to stay focused on the task at hand. What exacerbated my frustration was the fact that I was unsuccessfully trying to ignore the incessant whining of my talented muse, who desperately wanted to be anywhere but stuck indoors on this magnificent mountain day. I imagined my muse as some type of woodland nymph who wished she were outside romping around in the fragrant, piney woods with her fairy-winged friends.

Alas, I was saved from this exasperating internal struggle of wills by Sally returning home. When I went to the back door to greet her and help with the packages she would surely have, I noticed that she was getting out of the pickup more slowly than usual. Then I saw the reason why. She had a bundle in her arms. She carefully cradled it like a baby to her chest, and it was completely covered over with the lightweight fall jacket she always kept hanging in the truck as a spare. She seemed to be coddling something of considerable size. Oh Lord, I thought, what'd she bring home now? She was always bringing home some kind of wild orphan or injured critter. She and these unfortunate creatures had a habit of crossing paths.

"Come'ere!" came her call. "Come see what I found!" she exclaimed, with a huge mischievous grin and her eyes all atwinkle.

I rushed to the garden gate and opened it for her. "What've you got?"

When she cautiously separated the fabric of the jacket to make a small peephole, I peered into the warm darkness and spied a large bird. This was no mountain chickadee or little nuthatch. This was big. I couldn't quite see enough to make out its markings. "Oh, my god!" I whispered in amazement. "What is it?"

"I'm not sure. I think it's a female peregrine falcon. It's injured."

The thought sped across my mind that perhaps my muse had had some precognitive sense of what Sally encountered on her way home from town and I'd misinterpreted her reluctance to concentrate on our work as a desire to play. But that thought was quickly chased away by the many more urgent questions that began filling my head. "Where on earth did you find it? How did you catch it? What's wrong with it? Where are we going to put it?"

At this point, our Yorkies were beside themselves with curiosity. Yipping wildly, they'd charged out the door when I'd opened it and were now running and jumping around our feet trying to see what Sally had in her arms. They knew she had some living thing beneath that jacket, and they wanted to see what was emitting the feral scent of wildness that filled the air.

Our first order of business was to get the bird to a safe place, away from the dogs. We quickly moved into the cabin and down the basement stairs, leaving our little hunters upstairs behind the closed door. Then out the basement door and into the toolshed we went.

Sally handed me the warm bundle to hold while she lugged out the large dog carrier we had stored for just such an occasion. I cooed to the beautiful bird while I watched my friend scurry around to gather together the things she thought would make a comfortable temporary shelter for it. We knew how stressful it is for wild ones to be in such close contact with humans, and we understood the necessity of getting the falcon settled as quickly as possible. Sally hurriedly pulled up handfuls of the tall white tansy yarrow and fuchsia fireweed that grew on the sloping bank beyond the porch we stood under. She made a soft natural bed of these plants in the bottom of the carrier. Next she plucked a small log from the top of the woodpile and placed it over the bedding for a solid perch the bird could sink its talons into.

When Sally suddenly vanished back into the cabin, I gently stroked the bird's head and shoulders through the jacket, all the time speaking softly to it. I knew it must've been terribly frightened and so I tried to comfort it somewhat through calming touches and sounds. While I did this I thought about the laws that both Sally and I couldn't abide by, for it was deemed a crime to pick up any wild animal and a felony to harbor it in one's home, injured or not. The law stated that only an officially designated wildlife rescue person could handle wildlife. But in all good conscience, we paid these laws absolutely no heed, for we were always trying to save one kind of hurt animal or another. Actually, we were breaking the law even to feed deer and raccoons on our property, yet how are we to blame if these wild ones come to eat from the many bowls of feed we put out for the *birds*?

Our love of and compassion for all nature's wild ones leaves us no alternative to practicing quiet civil disobedience when it comes to this issue. We simply cannot drive on past an injured animal and switch off the deep compassion we feel for its suffering. Even if we spy a roadkill left by some hit-and-run driver, Sally will immediately hit the brakes and pull onto the shoulder. She will reach under the seat and don her extra set of gloves, get out, and gently move the unfortunate victim into the woods or roadside undergrowth, where it's out of sight and can have a little dignity in death.

At this point my thoughts were cut short by Sally's rushed return. She set containers of water and canned dog food in the carrier. It seemed to me that all was readied for the new occupant, and I made a motion to hand over the falcon to Sally. But she wasn't quite prepared to take it back. "Not yet," she said. "I need to try to clean out its eye. I think it may have collided with the road, there's dirt and gravel in it."

When I heard that my stomach sank. I felt so much sympathy for this poor bird.

Again I cooed to the injured wild one while we waited for Sally to gather more necessities. When she came back out of the cabin, she had a soft cloth and a bowl of warm water. I made sure that I had a firm grasp on both of the bird's feet with one hand while I gently pinned the wings beneath my arm. Slowly Sally peeled back the jacket to expose the falcon's beautiful head and then, very tenderly, she wiped away the dirt and gravel fragments from its huge eye. The bird didn't even wince. It just kept looking at her. It was as though it knew it was being helped–it knew. From the eye's red color we could see that there was internal bleeding, and after Sally thought she'd gotten its surface as clean as she could, I handed the falcon over to her.

Setting the bird down on the ground before the opened door of the carrier, Sally gently lifted the jacket off of it. The falcon hopped inside, and we shut and locked the door behind it.

I was now able to get my first good look at the bird. Ohh, what a magnificent beauty! From its facial markings this bird did indeed look like a female peregrine. In absolute wonder I watched as it stretched its wings. When it bent its neck to peer out at me, I looked at the injured eye and a great pity stung my heart.

"What are we going to do with it?" I asked.

My friend sighed. She wasn't sure of the answer. "We may have already done all we can. Getting it clean was the priority. The next thing we need to do is be sure we keep it in the dark. That eye's real bad. Sunlight will cause it intense pain." After she said that, Sally and I walked out into the sun and softly closed the shed door. "Let's leave it alone. It needs some quiet and darkness. This's been really stressful for it. The best thing for it now is to feel unthreatened so it can get some rest."

I wholeheartedly agreed. Now that the eye was clean, the wild one needed to calm down and rest from the trauma of being handled by two humans.

With that we went back into the cabin to calm our excited puppies and discuss our next move. Our first question was, Could a falcon, a hawk, or any bird of prey fly and hunt with an injured eye? Could a large bird of prey survive in the wild with just one good eye? We weren't sure of the answer, so Sally started calling around. Her first call was to a veterinarian in Colorado Springs who worked with wild birds. All she got from him was a tongue-lashing for picking up a falcon and taking it home. He was more interested in scolding Sally and making pseudothreatening noises about the strictness of the wildlife laws than in advising her on how to help the bird. Sally quickly had all she could take of his rambling ego and hung up on him.

Next she got on the Internet to search out specialized falconry organizations and then placed several calls to different ones across the country. In the end none of the so-called experts could agree. We weren't making much progress.

During her call to a Minnesota university that had a specialized research and rehab department for wild birds, Sally was asked to put the bird on a plane and fly it out to them so they could care for it. This was not an option. Not only was it too costly for us but we'd also be in hot water with the wildlife authorities for transporting an indigenous bird of prey out of the area.

When she called our county's sheriff department to get a referral to a local wildlife rescue center, she instead got "You picked up a *what*? You took a *what* to your *house*?" Sally explained that she wasn't intending to *keep* the bird, all she wanted to do was find the right place to *take* it for medical help and rehab. She was told to call the Woodland Park Forestry Department.

After several more calls we determined that we'd reached a "professional" answer to our question about the injured bird's ability to return to its natural habitat in such an impaired state. The "experts'" consensus was that a bird of prey could not survive in the wild with only one good eye. Its depth perception would be skewed and its flight balance thrown off. It was imperative that we find this falcon a new home where it would be fed, protected, and cared for until its eye had healed enough for it to be released into the wild.

Eventually, having spent hour after frustrating hour on the phone, we were given the name of a licensed wildlife rescue woman located on a road where I'd once lived. Sally called her and was asked to bring the bird over the following day. We were instructed to keep the bird in the dark (as it had been) and to transport it in a large cardboard box instead of the carrier. We were so relieved to hear that we'd done all the right things. In the meantime we continued keeping fresh water and meat in the carrier and left the bird alone so it wouldn't get overly stressed.

Now that the falcon's future was secure, Sally told me the story of how she found the bird. It'd been standing in the middle of our dirt road when she was returning from errands in Cripple Creek. She pulled off onto the shoulder, slowly got out of the truck, and spoke softly as she approached it. The bird flew a short distance and landed in some tall grasses. Since it was so uncharacteristic for a bird of prey not to quickly fly away from an approaching human, Sally investigated. She knew something had to be wrong with it and approached the bird again. That's when she saw its injured eye and knew it desperately needed human intervention to survive. So she returned to the truck and retrieved the spare jacket that she put over the bird.

The following day we transferred the falcon to a large cardboard box, which I held on my lap while Sally drove to the wildlife rescue place. We had a stop to make on the way. Sally had assured the woman who'd be caring for the bird that it would be no trouble at all to run an errand for her–to stop off at our vet's and pick up some injectable medication for one of the abandoned fawns she was caring for. Our vet, interested in what we had, came out to the truck to take a look at the falcon. He wished us luck with it. With full syringes in hand, Sally pointed the truck in the direction of Edlowe Road.

The wildlife rescue woman's name was Terri, and she was visibly pleased that Sally had cared enough to stop and try to save this beautiful bird. Her reaction, of course, ran counter to the letter of the law. It came from the heart, from the spirit of that law. After giving the bird a cursory examination and placing a dead mouse in its new cage, Terri informed us that she thought, with many months of care, the falcon had a chance of complete recovery. She went on to say that we could release the bird back where we found it after it was fully rehabilitated.

Then Terri showed us around her place, which was an animal lover's dream. She pointed out various large outdoor cages and what they held. One contained about seven or eight raccoon youngsters romping about. Hunters shoot the mothers hoping that the babies will die, Terri explained. She keeps the orphans and cares for them until they're old enough to be released back into the wild. Then Terri brought us up to a fenced area that held two small fawns whose mothers had also been shot. The prognosis for one was favorable, but she was dubious about the other. It was good to see the work Terri was doing to nurture these animals, but I was sad to hear that hunters were so often the ones responsible for making these poor animals orphans.

After our tour Terri looked at us curiously and grinned. "Since you two are so into saving wildlife, maybe you should look into getting your own licenses for doing this kind of work. You did a good job with the falcon. We could use more help." Sally and I just looked at each other, both thinking the thing we'd discussed so often–that there was so very much we wanted to do with this one lifetime we'd need clones of ourselves to get it all done! Yeah, we'd love to get wildlife rescue licenses and devote all our time to caring for injured and orphaned wild animals. What an absolutely wonderful and unconditionally loving job to have. Sigh. Ahh, yes, so many things we'd like to do and so little time . . . so very little time one lifetime holds. We shared our thoughts with Terri, concluding that we'd love to be licensed but we didn't have the time just now.

Months later, at the time of this writing, the falcon was still rehabilitating at Terri's place, where it was expected to enjoy a full recovery. A bird specialist had examined it and announced that what we delivered to the rehab center was not a female peregrine, as we and Terri had initially suspected, but a male prairie falcon. The specialist also concluded that the bird had been hit by a BB from a purposely aimed gun. It turned our stomachs to know that someone could have so little respect for life.

Before this book went to press Sally called Terri again to check on the falcon's progress. We were relieved when told of his complete recovery. Terri was sorry to inform us that she'd been advised by her superiors that it'd be better if his release was done somewhere other than where he was found . . . by someone other than us. Though we were disappointed to hear that we couldn't return the falcon to his familiar hunting grounds and have the heart-welling experience of seeing him healthy and flying free again, we were okay with it. Knowing that he was going to be fine was satisfaction enough. Our hearts were full just knowing we'd been instrumental in saving a beautiful, wild, wild life.

To that prairie falcon who was standing in the middle of a dusty dirt road, silently suffering from gravel and a BB in his eye, did Sally look like a threat or a blessing? Now that the falcon's eye is healed, does that grand bird have an inherent, instinctual sense that it'd been saved from certain death? These questions come to mind now and again. The answers are not clear to me. Perhaps animals have some subtle inner knowing of these things. Some level of acute perception that allows them to understand when they have been helped. I know that the scientific community would rail against such ideas. They'd laugh at me for even thinking such things. They'd jump to ridicule my anthropomorphization of animals. Scientific thought is oft an empty void bounded by touchable rigidness where *heart* plays no part and, if truth be told, is officially banned from the systemic method of discovery. Scientific thought needs to be liberated from its emotionally detached analytic objectivity when utilizing falsely conceptualized criteria for evaluation. The premise is false because it's glaringly incomplete. It's incomplete because it miserably fails to factor in the possibility that emotions and their elemental behavioral responses may not be the sole product of human elitism.

They–the scientific community–hold fast with a white-knuckled grip to the belief that animals possess no emotion, no sense of guilt, event recognition, or behavioral appreciation. And any scientific researcher who even hints at such a possibility is laughed out of the lecture halls and forever after perceived as one who voluntarily risked the credibility that validates her or his research.

It used to be that scientists all agreed that what separated humans from animals was the use of tools. This consensus went undisputed for decades . . . until Jane Goodall undeniably demonstrated that *chimpanzees use tools*! Not only do they use them but they use them creatively and effectively. So this little shocker rocked the scientific community. It rocked it like an off-the-scale seismic tremor, shaking the very foundations they'd built their weak theory on. But, being clever, those in the scientific community simply found a way around Jane's discovery. They'd gathered together to form a human column and, in a unified push for credibility, shoved the barrier defining the characteristic separating humans from animals a few inches to the other side of the formerly drawn line. They created a new theory to convince themselves that emotions–and the expression of and response to same–are a singularly human characteristic. Phooey! I've watched our puppies show more true emotion and a greater range of it than most humans I've known. I've felt their tenderly expressed love, their clearly exhibited appreciation. I've seen reactions depicting an ability to distinguish between a human's laughter generated from joy and the laughter of laughing "at" something, thereby creating a sense of humiliation in the animal.

Yes, I believe animals can feel humiliation. This I witnessed one day when one of our Yorkies had gotten tangled in some prickly brush and we had to shear her fur down nearly to the skin to get all the mats and burrs out. When we were done we made the rude mistake of laughing at how she looked. Hearing our laughter and seeing that we were doing it while looking down at her, our little dog immediately hung her head and, with her newly cropped tail drooping to the floor, slunk low to hide herself beneath the love seat. We tried to make up for our insensitivity, but no amount of upbeat coaxing or apologetic cajoling would ease her humiliation or her emotional pain. This little Yorkie had felt shame. It was so incredibly evident to us. She couldn't have expressed it more clearly if she could speak and tell us how thoughtless we were.

Similarly, our dogs' individualized expressions of jealousy can't be missed. The pure joy they demonstrate after you've found their long-lost favorite ball is unmistakable as well. The pouting sadness they display when you begin getting dressed for work is completely obvious. It tugs at your heart and makes you wish that you didn't have to leave the house. And, time and again, we've watched our dogs exhibit the dejected feelings of being left out. This last usually comes after Sally or I have given three of the dogs baths and are taking a rest. The fourth one will mope while staring at us with hopeful eyes as if to ask, "Did you forget about me?"

You can take all of those sheepskin documents and the claims that they represent intelligence, knowledge, and accomplishments. You can take them and use them to wrap fish in. The way I see it, they aren't worth an ounce of the greater wisdom that comes from simple observation and the clarity that comes from truly *seeing* what one is seeing, no matter how much it counters generally accepted theories expounded by the so-called experts.

I've repeatedly seen animals exhibiting emotions and widely varied behavioral responses. These responses haven't been demonstrated only by all the many pets I've cared for throughout my life; I've witnessed these behavioral characteristics in wildlife, too. From the raccoon family that comes to eat on our front porch at night to the mule deer bucks who come to drink from the birdbath, I've observed a wide range of behavioral traits that freely flowed forth from their own emotional well. So don't tell me that animals don't have emotions. Don't tell me that I'm a dreamer when I anthropomorphize them. Watch what you laugh at. Have a care about what you ridicule. Watch yourself because perhaps, just perhaps, it'll turn out that the humans are the ones who are being anthropomorphized when they emulate those who were on the planet before them. Perhaps the cavemen first used a tool *after* watching an ape break off a palm frond to use as a drinking cup.

Now that I've established that I've witnessed untold examples of animals exhibiting emotional responses, I'm returning to my initial ponderment: Did that falcon feel some subtle sense of appreciation for a human coming along and washing the damaging debris from its eye? Did it feel some gratefulness? Did it sense a blessing had come its way? Again, I reiterate that I can't definitively answer those questions. My best response would be that I honestly believe the rescued prairie falcon possibly *could* feel some of these things. He could indeed have felt a sense of appreciation for his pain being eased and then his being fed and cared for while he recuperated enough to be self-sufficient once again.

The one thing that the lettered pundits of the scientific community and I fully agree on is the fact that humans possess emotions and their resulting behavioral responses. We agree that humans can feel. They can feel through perception. People can feel awe, jealousy, joy, sadness, empathy, arrogance, pity, gratefulness, et cetera. Gratefulness. Gratefulness? This whole story is about gratefulness. It's about appreciating something good or wonderful that happened in one's life. Yet the emotional response that comes with gratefulness can't be felt unless that good "something" is first *recognized* as such. Those good and wonderful somethings that come our way are what we frequently call Blessings. Perhaps that falcon didn't recognize Sally coming along at a most propitious time in its life as being a Blessing. Perhaps it did. I tend to believe the latter. Yet there's no questioning or sitting on the proverbial fence about whether people have the capability to recognize the fortunate elements that fill every moment of their lives, from the glorious sunrise today to the golden daybreak that marks the fresh beginning of tomorrow. We already know that folks have the capability to perceive these good facets. The more critically pressing question is why so many people choose to be blind to them. Why? Why do so many people take their multiple blessings so much for granted that they never even see them?

This is the type of thing I spend time contemplating while I'm out alone in the deep woods. While the wind softly whispers through the sweetly scented high pines, the creek bubbles and gurgles its traveling song as a melodic backup to the singing feathered ones looking curiously down on their visitor. Within the simplicity of nature's ever-grounding innocence and pure beingness, the reasons for society's behavioral complexities and perceptual idiosyncrasies seem clearer. Here, Life is clearer, clarified by the very absence of the many visages of self-created, convoluted human thought and psychological labyrinths people tend to entangle their attitudes and world-view within. Here, in the rarefied mountain air that permeates nature's innocence, comes the simplistic answer to many of society's behavioral habits, even this one. Focus. That's the answer. People's focus. Their focus on life. We could also use the word *perspective,* yet *focus* is more defining and precise for this issue.

There seems to be a trend toward taking blessings for granted, not seeing them through one's eyes, mind, or heart. I've drawn this conclusion from the composite picture of the situation, which includes what people express verbally to me and what readers write to me. Attitudes I've heard and read from folks in many walks of life have demonstrated what I consider to be an across-the-board problem associated with recognizing one's blessings.

Basically, as I mentioned before, it comes down to focus. The focus people are tending to have is directed not toward their blessings but rather toward the negatives in their lives. These negatives capture people's daily focus because they're the problematical elements that have to be dealt with, those that cause stress and anxiety, and demand one's time in the search for immediate solutions. Whether these negatives be family or relationship difficulties or financial strains, they always seem to overshadow and smother all else in one's life. They always appear to darken one's days like an eclipse moving across the sun. And when this happens, the lights–the positive facets–in one's life are overlooked, ignored, and unappreciated. This focus on the trials of life dampens a person's natural spontaneity to express feelings of joy, elation, and gratefulness. When the dark clouds of negativity hang over one's mind, one's mood is correspondingly burdened with gloom that presses down on the shoulders like a wet woolen cloak. Consequently one shuffles around with slumped shoulders and a bent head–always looking down at the ground instead of up into the light of day, always focused on the shadows cast as one moves through time, not the sun that shines on one's back.

Negativity. It can often lead one headlong into a full-blown state of depression. Negativity is a singular focus on life's complications and troubles, its tribulations and setbacks. This negative cast on existence comes from viewing life through an incomplete perception–the skewed perception–that using only one eye will cause. It unbalances us. It's a blockage of sight but, unlike the falcon's, ours is voluntary. An outlook that takes in only the negative but not the positive doesn't provide the whole range of view. It's just a fraction of what's there to see and experience.

Those who focus on life's negatives–the One-eyed Jacks–will be those who mouth continual complaints. They have nothing positive to say. Their physical, spiritual, or emotional aches and pains will be all they can seem to speak of. Their money problems or troublesome familial relationships will fill their conversations. They'll be pulling a billowing thunderhead over themselves wherever they go. And others will cringe to see them coming.

So what would they see if these people decided to open both eyes and chose to stop being gloomy, glum One-eyed Jacks? Beautiful things. Glorious treasures! If a multitude of daily blessings aren't perceived, then one isn't seeing with both eyes. Life has polarity. It has negative and positive elements. Never only negative. Never solely positive. There is a fine balance. That balance is achieved through recognizing that, in reality, one's blessings far outweigh those lesser negatives. I just cannot fathom why anyone would prefer to drag a rain cloud around all the time. I just can't imagine how stuffy gloom can be more attractive than sweet joy. Maybe it's because folks don't really know what their blessings are. Could that be it? Could they truly not know that everything in their lives that isn't a problem is a blessing? Could it be that they really don't understand that every appliance that isn't broken is a blessing? That every day that goes by without having the flu is a blessing? That the health of their pet is a blessing? Gosh, could that be it?

Funny how quiet blessings often are. They just sit there happy, not making any fuss or mess to clean up, or causing any problems for the receiver. They don't scream, shout, or throw tight-fisted tantrums. They ask nothing and demand no one's time. They just . . . are. Like gleaming diamonds scattered among the sooty fragments of black coal hidden in a deep cavern, life's blessings exist beside the negatives. I wonder. I wonder why it is that people prefer to notice and hold on to only the darker pieces of life's experience, which sully their entire worldview. I wonder why they choose to ignore the sparkling treasures that surround them like twinkling dewdrops on a dawn-kissed magnolia blossom. I wonder at the folly of choosing to see only the negatives and voluntarily opting to turn one's head away from the gold in the stream of life. Seeing with both eyes, seeing life's balanced polarity with both eyes wide open is a clear personal choice. And I wonder why folks don't choose joy over gloom.

I wonder. I wonder because the prairie falcon had no choice, it had no such choice to make for itself. Humans do have that choice to make . . . and most won't. Yet there are many who will choose the easier, more joy-filled option.

I believe one of the main reasons folks don't immediately recognize their many blessings is the increasing complexity of daily life. The pace of the twenty-first century has dramatically quickened. Business is conducted on cell phones while driving the kids to school and walking the golf course greens. The vast network of information available on the Internet keeps eyes glued to monitor screens. When we need to move from here to there, it's with an almost frenetic haste. Haste and distractions. No wonder the simple elements of life are so readily overlooked.

That taxi that just happened to appear out of nowhere when you needed it so desperately wasn't the result of merely being lucky like you thought. It was a blessing to count.

The lightning strike that hit your phone line and left your computer intact wasn't simply a "close call." It was a blessing in your life.

Those afternoon showers that you complain about are a blessing when the rest of the country is in a drought or when forest fires are blazing in other states.

There's so much we take for granted, so much that lies beneath the complexities of our daily living that oftentimes the simple things are overwhelmed by an all-consuming perspective of the Greater. Unknowingly, we mentally classify all external stimuli along the measuring points of a graduated scale of importance. The small stuff goes unnoticed while those factors carrying greater impact are given our prioritized attention. That small stuff gets its due time only when it goes awry and causes problems. Yet when it plods along according to plan, it's ignored and never recognized as a blessing.

See all your blessings for what they are. Don't sweat the small stuff–be thankful for it!

feral orphans—respect for life

MOUNTAINS, REMOTE AND SECLUDED. Mountains, wild and raw.

The high Rocky Mountains, full of prowling cougars, howling coyote packs, darting red foxes, keen-eyed owls, hungry black bears, and . . . newborn kittens.

The above statements are all true. The above statements are facts of life. The first and second are givens, but the last element of the third statement isn't a given and shouldn't be. That element is the product of human beings with no respect for life, no conscience when it comes to quickly getting small unwanted animals off their hands, no compassion for those tiny lives, and no personal responsibility or integrity whatsoever. It's a fact of life that people drive up into the more remote regions of these mountains every year and drop thousands of helpless kittens and puppies into the wilds. The circuitry of my brain smokes and then short-circuits every time I try to reason out the situation. It short-circuits because there is no rationale. None. Nada. Nyet. None whatsoever.

Many people aren't aware of the thousands of domesticated animals abandoned each year in the rural areas of this country, because most folks don't often leave the cities where they live. They have homes in the city or suburbs, shop within their municipalities' perimeter, and their friends usually live within the city as well. Sometimes the holidays take them out of the urban areas they know well and up into the mountains. But even then the casual vacationer is mainly interested in getting some much deserved quiet and relaxation away from work, time to take in the panoramas of spectacular scenery, leisure spent soothing weary bones and mind in rejuvenating hot spring waters, time sitting in a boat in the middle of an alpine lake with visions of the "big one" teasingly dancing before his mind's eye, or maybe even moseying along the well-worn paths of a dude ranch's trail ride. These vacationers come up to the mountains for a short span of time. They ride the surface of the lake water without getting their feet wet. They scan the wide-angle view of panoramic vistas, seeing the treetops lining the many ridges without noticing the starwort growing on the forest floor. At best, their experience of the mountains is a cursory one, and there's nothing wrong with that. People need to get away from the day-to-day grind of their nine-to-fives. They need a relaxing break. What I'm getting at is the fact that unless one actually lives up in those mountains some elements of them can't be known. It takes someone who's lived in those hills for a good amount of time to understand the extent of particular situations in those remote regions. People dumping small domesticated animals in the high forested wilds is one of those situations.

Since moving to Colorado I've lived in a total of eleven mountain dwellings. Each of these places was visited by its own particular species of wild creatures. Families of black bear lived nearby several of them. Some were frequented by packs of coyotes. Three were on property that cougar claimed as their roaming range. From most of them I saw foxes, mule deer, or elk. Raccoons stopped by each and every mountain house where I lived. And *all* the properties had stray *puppies and kittens.* Imagine! Just imagine how many tiny kittens and puppies there are in these mountains if they were coming out of the woods surrounding all eleven of the dwellings I lived in. All eleven of them! Why, when you think about that it's nothing less than astounding. How can humans be so cruel as to dump these wee, helpless bits of living fluff into wilds full of predators and extremely harsh weather elements? It's like dropping a squirming mouse into the cage of a hungry snake! I simply cannot fathom the total lack of compassion of people who do this. They must be coldhearted to dump these poor creatures out where they'll surely starve, freeze, or experience excruciating pain as they're torn apart by owls, pumas, or coyotes. Why can't people simply take these unwanted pups or kittens to their local Humane Society? At least in an animal shelter these animals have some chance of being adopted. At least there they'll be given a humane injection if they're not adopted.

Our vet informed us that only two species of domesticated animals–horses and cats–can survive in the wild. If an older dog is abandoned, it may survive if it gains acceptance by a coyote pack, but this is more the exception than the rule. Abandoned puppies are a lost cause. They quickly become some predator's meal. The kittens have a better chance if they stay together or are quickly taught survival techniques by their feral mother. Older cats usually adapt well to the wild unless they're sick or injured, impairing their hunting ability. Healthy cats are excellent hunters.

That brings me to the second concern abandoned animals raise. Healthy adult domesticated felines who are dumped off in the mountains are upsetting the balance of mountain wildlife. There are now so many feral cats killing for their sustenance that they are decimating entire species of rodents and birds. These once cuddly household pets become feral orphans who must quickly adapt in order to survive in their new harsh surroundings. They accomplish this by falling back on their hunting instincts. And, suddenly, nature is thrown out of calibration.

One of our homes was a little stone cabin, surrounded by heavy pine and aspen woods, that happened to have windows with very low sills. Each evening I'd sit in my reading chair next to one of these windows and work on my writings. Around about the time when the dusky light of twilight hit each of the windows, I began noticing that a cat kept coming to check out the dogs' outside water bowl. I watched it drink and drink. Thereafter, I kept an eye out for it and noticed that it liked to huddle at the bottom of the many-branched lilac tree growing at the edge of one of the windows. Sally and I felt sorry for the small orphan, so the next time we went grocery shopping we added cans of cat food to our cart. We started leaving a bowl of it beneath the lilac. Nightly the cat would eat the food we set out, but it was so wild and wary that it would have nothing to do with us.

The cat grew fatter, and we soon realized she was pregnant. The snow began to fall, and we were increasingly concerned when days passed without the expectant mama coming to eat. We looked for her tracks around the cabin and in the nearby forest but found none. Then one evening a movement in the yard caught my attention. I looked closely and saw the cat; the moonlight had glinted off her eye when she came to the bowl, which, by the way, we never stopped filling for her. She was ravenous and left not a speck of food behind.

Night after night Mama came. We suspected she'd lost her babies to predators since she always came alone. But one evening, to our great surprise, more than one shadow moved by the moonlit bowl. The smaller shadows scampered and tumbled about in the fresh snow. These curious, wee and fluffy shadows soon leapt onto the cabin window's low ledge to discover what kind of strange wild creature was peeking out at them.

"B–babies!" I excitedly sputtered as Sally sat at the kitchen table working on art for one of my books. "Come see! She brought her babies! They're okay!" My friend rushed to the window and said she was relieved to know that Mama's litter was a fine healthy one. Then she spun around and went to the cupboard to fill two more bowls of cat food for the new family. I watched as she took them outside. Seeing a human come, Mama immediately dashed off. One by one the kittens scampered after her.

That night Sally and I discussed what we should do about this family of visitors. It was a dilemma. We naturally felt compassion for the abandoned mother and her five tiny kittens. But we also knew that these sweet kittens were going to be forced to mature before their time. The normal luxury of spending hour upon hour playing with a ball of string would never be theirs. Their hours were a predetermined destiny . . . that of quick courses in becoming feral. Each one was going to become a skilled hunter that would bring down untold numbers of birds, chipmunks, squirrels, and even rabbits. Each of those five kittens was going to grow into adulthood and produce more feral offspring, which would, in turn, do the same. This was a vicious cycle that was being repeated over and over again throughout the mountains. We couldn't do anything about all of those other wild places it was occurring, but we knew that there had to be something we could do about it happening right in the middle of our own little corner of the forest.

Catch 'em! That was what we'd do. After all, they were just tiny kittens, for heaven's sake. They were just little pieces of fluff, weren't they? How hard could it be?

As it turned out, it was no simple task. Mama had been an excellent teacher from day one. No way were those little scampering tykes going to let a human being get anywhere near them–and *absolutely* no way were they going to let *two* of those two-legged creatures get within thirty feet of them! If Sally and I didn't look like two sillies trying to catch a little kitten, I don't know what we looked like. We managed to capture one before they wised up. Just one. Still, that was one less to grow up and become a predator. That was one less left in the wilds to give birth to more hunters. As young as the kitten we caught was, it was already well on its way to becoming feral. Its mama had done a superior teaching job. It hissed and clawed. Clawed and hissed. But after a few days with us it did settle down. The constant availability of a food source was our most useful means of persuasion. And our reluctant houseguest grew more amenable after it decided it liked being cooed to and petted while enjoying the radiating warmth of the cabin's woodstove fire.

We took our furry visitor for a vet check to make sure there was nothing wrong with it before we attempted to place it in a permanent home. Our veterinarian assured us that the kitten was in good health, no diseases or fleas, no ticks or any other negative conditions were evident from being birthed in the wilds. This was good news. It took us only a short time to find someone who wanted to give it a good home. One wild kitten saved from a hard, feral life, and thousands of birds and chippers given a reprieve.

When Sally and I moved into our current cabin, which is even more secluded than the stone one was, so many birds began coming to our feeders that the place looked like a bird sanctuary. One day we counted thirteen species of birds that were either feeding on the porch or waiting in the trees for their turn. Clark's nutcrackers, two kinds of woodpeckers, two kinds of juncos and chickadees. We have flocks of big crows, raucous ravens, and tiny nuthatches. Gray jays and Steller's jays. To our surprise we even saw an Eastern blue jay, a cedar waxwing, and an American goldfinch in one day. We had so many doves that a package delivery woman pulled her truck down our drive and, with amazement, asked me if we had a dovecote. Flocks of band-tailed pigeons started arriving around Mother's Day and staying through the warm months. They began routinely summering here and always have a prolific breeding season.

Right around the time when the snow begins to get serious–usually the middle of November–thousands of rosy finches come to perch in the bare aspens. They sound like hail when they land on the wooden planks of the porch while they're feeding. The little snowbirds are particularly interesting to me because I never spy them unless there's new-fallen snow on the ground. They obviously have an apt name, but where on earth do they come from? Where are they when there's no snow? Curious little birds. Curious how they come with the snowfall. We also had a sharp-shinned hawk appear and hang out in the aspens in front of the porch for several days; Sally got some spectacular photographs of it. Other regular feathered visitors are red-winged blackbirds, red crossbills, pine grosbeaks, cowbirds, redpoll finches and, of course, dozens of little pine siskins. We're also blessed with four pair of beautiful magpies, a resident saw-whet owl, and two pair of great horned owls. Word seems to have gotten around the bird world that our cabin is *the* place to get free grub. We now have to buy two hundred pounds of sunflower seed and cracked corn twice a month or the bird diner's cupboards will be bare. The folks up at the feed store love us. In fact, they commented that our huge flocks of birds were so unusual, they displayed our photos of them on their store bulletin board. The old-timers coming into the store are amazed when they see the variety and amount of birds visiting us.

So we'd moved into this secluded cabin, put seed out, and the birds came. They came one by one, then flock by flock. In droves they came. So did the cats. Four of them. And we'd run outside and chase them away. We'd shoot our .38s and .22s into the air, hoping the noise would frighten them away (we never aimed at them). This technique scared off three of the feral cats. But the holdout would not be threatened or run out of Dodge. What to do? What indeed, for we were finding rosy finch and yellow pine siskin wings around the bottom of the woodpile. Once Sally came into the house holding a freshly killed cedar waxwing. It'd just happened. We'd actually seen the cat jumping up on the porch rail to snatch away a fluttering finch while dozens were there feeding. When Sally cleaned out the toolshed one spring day she gagged from coming across the massive bed of bird feathers the cat had made itself. By then we were just plain sick and tired of finding the beautiful pink finch wings lying around. We had to do something. All of these birds had created a safe sanctuary for themselves, and here was this silent predator lying in wait for the choicest pickin's. A predator that never really had to hunt, only patiently lie in wait for the food to come to it.

We initially reasoned that if we fed the cat and kept its

belly full it would be less inclined to hunt and kill. Wrong. No matter how much cat food we put out, the bowl would be licked clean and we'd still find just as many wings scattered about. The cat's hunting instincts were just too strong. Clearly it hunted and killed for pure sport.

During our ongoing search for a viable solution to our feral cat problem we discovered a clever little something called a Havahart. This is a humane trap that comes in various sizes. Our second ingenious plan was to catch the feline hunter in one of these traps and release it on a friend's ranch, where the cat could happly live out its life in a barn. We didn't waste any time ordering one of these contraptions from the feed store and, a week later, picked it up. With visions of guaranteed success dancing in our heads, we placed a bowl of cat food inside the device.

We waited.

And waited.

Every morning we eagerly checked the trap–nothing there.

Then, a few mornings later, we found that the bowl inside the trap had been licked clean, but no cat. We'd set the trap wrong. We rebaited it and waited again. When we checked the trap this time–success! The cat was inside! Yea! Our birds were safe again! Sally placed the trapped prize in the back of the pickup, and down the drive she went. She hit a bump, the trap tipped, the cat slipped out and shot into the woods. Sigh.

Again we baited the trap.

And again we waited.

And waited.

But the cat was far too clever for us. It had learned its lesson well. It would not go into that trap no matter what sort of bait we put inside. And again we began finding bird wings beneath the porch.

When we took our Yorkies to the vet the following week to get their annual shots, Sally told him about the cat that was killing our birds and how all of our ground squirrels and chippers had also vanished. She asked him if veterinarians ever neutered feral cats or put them to sleep if someone took the time to catch them and bring them in. Our vet told us that no animal doctor he knew would even want to handle a feral cat, let alone operate on one or give it an injection. He then shared some more disturbing facts about feral cats in our mountains. They decimate the ground squirrel and chipmunk populations and have completely wiped out some bird species. He informed us that people from the cities come up to the mountains and leave their unwanted pets. They do it at an alarming rate. The local pounds are overflowing. The volunteer animal rescue folks are overworked trying to find homes for the abandoned dogs. And the cats are so numerous that they're actually upsetting the balance of nature.

Hearing all of this was sobering. Sally and I looked at our vet, then at each other. When our eyes again met his, his solution was clear and unspoken. Not being one to leave things open to possible misinterpretation, Sally hesitantly voiced the question we were both thinking, "So, so what're you saying? We *shoot* them?"

The vet raised one confirming brow and sighed.

Oh God. My heart plummeted to my stomach while I listened to him explain. "It's not something folks readily talk about but, yes, everybody does it. There's just no other way. Once a feral cat, always a feral cat."

Then we sighed. What a crummy, rotten damned solution we were handed. Right then I despised the inhumanity of humans. I hated their apathy toward their unwanted pets. I hated their lack of compassion and their laziness and their gross lack of personal responsibility for small bits of life they didn't want to have to deal with anymore. I hated the fact that all of that combined inhumanity was suddenly dropped in our laps. Now it was up to us to put an end to the wildlife deaths in our own backyard.

Sally and I didn't talk much on the way home from the vet's. Neither of us wanted to admit that the generally resorted-to solution–the never spoken about solution–was the only one, yet we both knew . . . we knew. We knew because we'd explored all other options.

As it happened, our reluctance to act on this solution immediately was a blessing for all concerned. Luckily, we'd mentioned our problem to a neighbor who suggested we make one last effort to catch the cat . . . with a fresh, whole fish. She didn't think the feline would be able to resist such a tempting bait. This last-ditch idea was certainly worth a try. We clung to the thread of possibility that there was one slim alternative to taking the cat's life. It worked! The cat was drawn to the fish on the first night, and Sally successfully released it on a rancher's land where the multiple barns provided shelter and sustenance by way of their excess rodent population. A great sense of relief washed over us. Now our flocks of birds were once again safe in their sanctuary. The following year, squirrels returned to feed on the porch and the chipmunk burrows were occupied by new families. Word got around the wildlife kingdom that the feeders, grounds, and burrows here were safe again.

Before the appearance of these feral cats, before witnessing firsthand the massive, stomach-churning remnants from just one cat's weekly kills, we would never have known about the incredible problem feral cats were causing in the beautiful wilds of nature. We would never have known what was the most unexpected unnatural predator. The one that so effectively threw nature off balance. A lot of killing has to be going on to throw nature off like that–a *lot.* And if once-domesticated house cats are doing it, where are their former owners? The cats' natural hunting instincts kick in when they're forced to depend on these ingrained skills. Who forced these cats to resort to those instincts? Who suddenly took away their warm and comfy homes? Who stopped setting daily bowls of food out for them? Who stole away their sunny windowsill seats and replaced them with the cold, harsh woods? Who is responsible for thousands of wildlife deaths because they stopped caring and having a conscience about a pet's life? Who is responsible for condemning that pet to a life of being an indiscriminate killer? Sally and I know. So do you. We all know who is responsible. Question is . . . Why? I would more pointedly ask . . . How?

How on earth can a human being be so heartless as to take a family pet that is accustomed to its sheltered comforts and meals and dump it out in the wild woods or on a deserted country road? That human being can have no respect for life. And that lack of respect for life is scary.

It's clear to see that a lack of respect for human life often follows a lack of respect for animal life. Many forensic psychologists, profilers, and criminologists will testify that untold numbers of adult murderers have a childhood and/or adolescent history of exhibiting cruelty to animals. The offending individuals come to believe that they have control over life and death. As youths these people find that the exhilaration of executing animals becomes an addictive high. Eventually the killing of helpless animals is no longer the challenge and thrill it once was, and the perpetrators cast their eyes about for more interesting, human victims.

It would be ridiculous to imply that everyone who dumps the family pet into a secluded forest is a potential murderer. So let me make it clear at the outset that I'm not saying that at all.

What I am saying is that both the murderer and the individual who leaves a family pet in the wild have no respect for life. The owner who abandons a pet may vehemently defend his or her actions, yet the arguments will be riddled with groundless rationalizations. There are no rational reasons not to place a pet that is no longer wanted at an animal shelter, with the Humane Society, or in a good home.

The most commonly heard rationales go something like this: "It's just an animal." Or "I didn't know what else to do." And "Cats love to hunt anyways." Let's take a look at the first statement. It's just an animal. It seems to me that if animals are such an inconsequential element of our world, humans must be even less valuable because God made the animals first. God thought of populating the earth with all manner of animals before the idea of humans popped into the divine mind. We were thought of last . . . an afterthought perhaps? Though it'd be highly arrogant to speculate what was in God's mind at the time of Creation, we do know that, historically, all highly spiritual individuals have loved God's creatures. These revered people inherently recognized and felt animals' specialness, their uniqueness, their ordered place within multispecies Creation, for no living thing was created without purpose. The problem is that many humans today are incredibly shortsighted. They have no idea that such a grand purpose could be connected with the family's furry hamster, ferret, cat, or parakeet. Yet all have precious life. All have beating hearts. All have emotions and personality. All have beingness. And when the life within a life, even within a tiny animal's life, isn't perceived as being valuable, respect is no longer associated with that life.

We're human beings. That's all we are. So who are we to point a finger at this or that species of life and declare one more important or valuable than the other? Who are we to suppose that we can cruelly mistreat an animal or condemn one to a life of hardship or slow starvation? Do humans feel they can judge creatures this way because they believe they're now the species who has might over all others? Is it because there are no longer animal predators out there to best us? To hunt us? Speculation, I know, yet the fact remains that all creatures first existed as a thought within the mind of God. And if God thinks of them with enough respect to create them, shouldn't we think of them with enough respect to care for them?

The second excuse was this: "I didn't know what else to do." Oh, get real, for heaven's sake. Even the four-year-old tyke next door has heard of Humane Societies. Or what about placing an ad in the paper for a no-longer-wanted family pet? What about posting a "Free-to-Good-Home" notice at the vet's office, at the grocery store, or at work? Or asking friends and neighbors? The person who abandons a pet and gives lame excuses only makes himself or herself look more the fool and ignorant of the many obvious options that are available.

This second excuse comes with an underlying, unvoiced inference–"I didn't have to take *responsibility* for my actions because I was ignorant. I didn't know any better." This excuse is a cover-up for something that runs in a current far deeper than simple ignorance. It makes ignorance the scapegoat. Few folks will believe that the person didn't know any better. Instead, many will recognize this statement's underlying truth–the person who utters such words refuses to expend a bit of time and energy to find the pet a new home. An animal, especially a domesticated one, is not a piece of unwanted furniture or some inanimate knickknack one drops off in a Goodwill box in the dark of night without another thought. Society makes accommodations for animals. It provides places of care for these lives God put here on earth. Society recognized the need to supply shelters where unwanted animals can be fed, housed, and, we hope, adopted back into loving homes by people who appreciate the fact that they can save a life. Saying that you didn't know what else to do is like saying you don't know what a spoon is for while eating soup with your fingers. It sounds ridiculously ignorant. To use this excuse as a reason for dumping a family pet into the wilds multiplies that ignorance a thousandfold.

The third excuse–"Cats love to hunt anyways"–is based on a feline's basic instincts. Okay, that's true. Anyone who's ever had a house cat will agree that the statement is a given. The family cat will even hunt a moving shadow. It'll crouch, silently move toward it, and then, in a flash of fur, pounce on it. Cats will stalk nearly anything that moves, especially if that moving thing peeps or squeaks. But this excuse is pitifully poor human logic when applied to the wilds, for domesticated felines were never meant to live in the forests and on country lanes. When cats are suddenly dumped there, the resident furry and feathered lives that make those wilds their home are the ones that suffer and die.

Though cats are excellent hunters, the idea that they will easily survive in the wilds because of their natural instincts is logic without heart. It's using a known fact without applying the exponential ramifications. It's using knowledge without the depth of wisdom. And acting on knowledge without wisdom is a very dangerous thing to do. That incomplete thought process never considers what the abandoned cat's *prey* will be.

Prey. We've gotten down to the cat's prey. So this single dumped-off feline may brunch on a few field mice and perhaps make supper out of a couple of birds. Big deal. There are lots of mice and birds out in the wild anyway. Right? Read my lips–a singular negative never makes a positive. What does that mean? It means that the owner of the unwanted cat thinks he or she is introducing only *one* feline into the wild and, after all, what difference could that possibly make to the nature of things–to the nature of nature? The owner falsely reasons that one little cat, like the single drop of industrial waste dropped into a clear stream, couldn't possibly hurt anything. Yet that owner doesn't stop to consider that his neighbor, that neighbor's neighbor, the grocer around the corner, his uncle, his uncle's neighbor, and that neighbor's neighbor have also dumped cats out in the wild. Suddenly that one drop of industrial waste has become a bucketful, the bucketful has turned into gallons, the gallons have turned into a steady piped-in flow.

A single negative will always leave its mark. And so we have hundreds of cats being abandoned in the wild every year. A single cat can hunt and kill hundreds of chipmunks, squirrels, rabbits, and birds in a year. Just one cat. And it does this not because it's starving but because it has the inherent instinct to kill. It does this because it can. Hunting and killing prey is ingrained in its nature. More often than not hunting is pure sport for a cat. Multiply the kills of one cat by hundreds of annually abandoned felines and what do you have? This is no riddle. What we end up with is a pandemic of feral felines loosed on nature. What we end up with is mountain residents being forced into the heartbreaking situation of having to deal with the problem. All because some human, his neighbor, his neighbor's neighbor, his uncle, his uncle's neighbor didn't apply wisdom or logic to knowledge, because they had no respect for life.

The abandonment of domestic pets in the wild is a shadowy, malevolent beginning of something far worse; it is a tiny malignant seed of unconscionable behavior. In children we see this behavior sprout into a disrespect for life when they so casually take a gun and shoot another child for his designer shoes. We see it when children aim a gun at another youngster who is wearing the wrong colors. We see it in drive-by shootings where the one with the gun doesn't even know who's being brought down. We see it when children are cruel to their pets or find some twisted thrill in pulling wings off of butterflies. And we see it full-blown in adults who find murder the solution to a life problem, who are involved in terrorist groups, who practice apartheid, who are fascinated by snuff films.

I don't need to keep giving examples. The nightly newscasts do that already. They do that in graphic Technicolor. They, in turn, exacerbate the situation by using these stories as headliners to hook their tragedy-obsessed audience. You may think I'm making a tremendous leap from dumping domesticated cats out in the woods to watching snuff films, but you'd be wrong. The disrespect for life doesn't begin with those films–it began far earlier in life, it began as a small seed and grew into something distorted and ugly.

I don't understand this lack of respect for life–be it human or animal. This old mind of mine simply cannot compute how anyone can lack a solid respect for all living things. Why people's minds don't seem to have knowledge of the preciousness of life within the smallest animal or why their hearts don't seem to be touched by a small life's beautifully undulating energies is incomprehensible to me. I don't understand why some people tend to equate Life value with only human life. All life-forms are interdependent, and humans depend *more* upon the other animal and botanical species than they on us.

Every living thing on this precious, beautiful planet of ours vibrates with the shining essence of life and sings pure and clear with uniquely exquisite energy. Every living thing upon this magnificent planet joins its separate vibrations to unite as a sacred Choir of Creation that manifests a softly chanted Hum of Life echoing Grandmother Earth's own steady heartbeat.

Please, if you should have an unwanted pet, please take it to a shelter instead of ever entertaining the thought of abandoning it. To abandon a pet is to condemn thousands of innocent wild lives. All problems have multiple choices of resolution; some of these solutions are clearly wrong when fully analyzed. Every single act one performs, no matter how small, is like a ship at sea collecting barnacles as it moves through the waters of life because *every act creates a reaction.* The individual who dumped a cat out in the wild is of the mind that that's the end of his or her problem, yet it's only the beginning of the problem for nature. When thinking we've found a good solution to a particular situation, we need to widen our perspective beyond self. We need to ask questions of ourselves about that intended solution. What effects will this solution leave on others, on society, on relationships, on nature? Think further than your own limited spatial bounds. Think further, especially when a life is involved . . . even the family pet's. Please, please think further.

hour of the bear—acceptance

"LIONS AND TIGERS AND BEARS!" YOU KNOW the rest.

Mountain lions roamed the woods around three of the houses where I have lived. They occasionally checked out the place, venturing close enough to leave their telltale muddy paw prints across the planks of the deck.

I've never had tigers in any of the forests I've lived in unless, of course, they were of the small, domesticated feline variety gone feral.

And bears. Bears have lived almost everywhere I have. Black bears. I've seen black bears that were ebony-colored, just like a person would expect black bears to look, as well as black bears that came in coat colors ranging from a dark chocolate truffle to auburn-touched cinnamon. Papa bears and mamas with a roly-poly cub or two scampering close behind them. In a forest deep or on a cabin porch, bears abound everywhere in Colorado's piney wilds.

I really don't suppose that anyone who makes a home in a forest can go for long without crossing paths with a bear, at least spying one. Whether that home be a remote, rustic cabin or a six-bedroom place in an upscale residential community, bears are going to be a fact of life. At one time or another they're going to announce their presence as neighbors. And whether the house dweller likes it or not, the furry neighbors are there to stay. Some folks believe this situation isn't very neighborly. And I guess that's the problem. A problem arising from human fear rather than respect.

My former cabin was a tiny stone place tucked back off a dead-end dirt road in a rather large residential mountain community. The cabin was the only dwelling on the road and was surrounded by heavily forested land. Even in full daylight herds of mule deer came to feed fifteen feet from the front windows. Raccoons came nearly every night. And my companion and I lived a peaceful coexistence with these different children of the Old Woman of the Woods.

At the end of August 1995, shortly after we returned from a monthlong cross-country book-signing tour, we were relaxing one evening in the living room illumined only by the soft glow of a couple votive candles. The window blinds were open, and we were sitting in silence, just enjoying the quiet aura of our shared companionship and, once in a while, gazing outside to see if any deer or raccoons were meandering into the beams of the exterior floodlights. Something dark moved along the bottom of the low window ledge and, not immediately recognizing its form, we both got up for a better look. As we reached the window and peered down, we saw that our visitor was a bear.

The bear stopped sniffing along the foundation and stood up to its full height on two legs. We were nose to nose with it. We were nose to nose with a bear and only double-paned glass separated it from us. Though we were shadowed in the semidarkness of the interior, the bear still saw us. Sally grabbed the back of my shirt and yanked me away from the window. Our dogs began barking up a storm, and the bear dropped onto all fours, turned, and ambled off into the woods. A short time later Mr. and Mrs. Raccoon came to feed. This, we knew, was nature's all-clear sign. The bear had left the area. He made return trips throughout that fall and again the following spring and summer. That summer was when we'd heard that, in a distant part of the mountain subdivision, a resident had shot a bear that had attacked his dogs. Ours was not the only place being visited by bears, and there is no reason to believe that our visitor isn't still casing the little stone place to this very day. But I couldn't say for sure because we relocated to an even more secluded cabin the following summer.

The visitation by bears was not the reason we relocated. To think one can live in the woods and be free from the possibility of bears dropping by is ludicrous. We relocated because my real estate friend had found the place she knew I'd always been looking for and also had a buyer for my stone cottage (which, by the way, wasn't even for sale then). To make a long story very short, the stone place sold before the ink on the listing papers was dry, and Sally and I closed on an unfinished cedar cabin overlooking a secluded, picturesque valley. We were miles and miles away from any of the more popular residential subdivisions. The only road around us was our own driveway snaking through a forest and dead-ending at our little homestead. No electricity. No other dwellings. No neighbors. No neighbors except for the furred and feathered ones, the raccoons, coyotes, foxes, chippers, birds, and . . . bears.

Black bears came around at all hours of the day and night. We thought it an oddity for them to show up in the mornings and also on sunny afternoons when we were out working around the property. We initially attributed this unusually bold bear behavior to the fact that our new place had never been lived in full-time. It'd been built as a weekend construction project. On the whole, the place had been left uninhabited for nearly thirteen years. So, we figured that the wildlife in the area weren't used to seeing humans or dogs around on a daily basis.

Mule deer bucks with magnificent, prize-sized antlers would come and stand in the lower drive and watch me stack the wood that Sally was busy splitting. The deer stood on the crest of the bank behind the cabin while my companion's chain saw shattered the silence and my wheelbarrow bumped and rumbled along the gravel drive. We came to realize that every time we were outside, whether stacking wood, staining the exterior of the cabin, laying railroad-tie steps, or planting flowers in the garden area, eyes were watching us. There were always watchers out there. And one day the watcher was a bear. Not wanting to press our luck, we casually set our tools down and went inside, where we discussed the new visitor.

Sally told me about the times she'd been out in the forest felling dead standing trees and the hair on the back of her neck would bristle. She admitted that her first thought in such instances was that a bear was near, and she'd shut off the chain saw and drive her load back down to the house. Bears and the possibility of a wood-cutting accident were the two main dangers that had recently prompted us to invest in a couple of transceivers. Sally was occasionally out in the woods working alone, and with these simple emergency communicators she and I could talk to each other clearly anywhere within the bounds of our property. We agreed now that they were indeed a wise purchase.

Now that the bear had come to check out our home, we wondered just how far its curiosity would take it. Would it simply look us over and then be on its way? Would it eye our small Yorkies and file the thought of them away for a future time when it was really hungry? Would it consider us a threat or view us as somewhat of an innocuous nuisance to be tolerated in its domain? After all, we were making quite a racket in its woods. That first day the bear came we watched it from inside the house until it ambled off. Soon afterward, we returned to our work. What the incident taught us was to always be acutely aware of our surroundings, even when we were working within twenty or thirty feet from the house.

Every year the Colorado Springs and Denver television news reporters broadcast stories of bears going into people's rural yards or even venturing into towns. This is not a bit unusual to hear about. And, we discovered, it was not going to be unusual for us either. To assist people in discouraging these bear visitations, the newsfolks annually emphasized the importance of keeping one's barbecue grill thoroughly cleaned of meat grease and other cookout residue, firmly securing the lids of all garbage and trash cans, taking all food out of vehicles that are not parked in garages, never leaving dogs' bowls out at night, and, the biggie, not hanging hummingbird feeders or any other types of bird feeders around the house. Oh right. This last cautionary rule was a joke to us because of the way the huge variety of birds had made our cabin their sanctuary. There was just no way we were going to stop feeding our feathered friends once they'd come to rely on our place as one of their main migratory stopovers. Were we suddenly going to take away their café? Dismantle their comfy, well-stocked local hangout? No way!

Feed the birds and the raccoons come to eat.

Feed the birds and the deer come to eat.

Feed the birds and the bears come to eat.

Feeding the birds drew every woodland critter within a mile around.

To us this was just the way it was.

Though we were primarily intending to invite birds, chippers, and squirrels, we knew the Uninvited would also come to partake of our simple table offerings. There was no way around it. Nope. No way, no how. So, in the backs of our minds, where reality couldn't hide, we came to expect the unexpected. We couldn't turn away the little critters for fear of the larger ones possibly wanting to sample the tasty, easy feast. We didn't have long to wait for the one party crasher we knew would eventually turn up again.

The bear appeared during one brightly moonlit evening when we were sitting in the living room having a light conversation. The valley-facing picture window blinds were open wide as usual because we liked to watch the moon arc across the pane. Sally, sitting nearest the glass, commented that we had a large raccoon on the porch, and she got up to peek at it. Our coons are personality plus and have easily accepted our presence on the other side of the glass while they eat from the food bowls and feeders. When we went over to the window, our eyes widened to see the huge size of this raccoon's back as it moseyed on all fours with its nose to the porch planks.

This was no coon, it was a bear!

And again, as had happened in the stone cottage, the bear caught sight of us and rose on his back legs. Again Sally grabbed hold of my shirt and yanked me away from the glass. Before she could lower the blind, the bear had scampered down the steps and lumbered up the drive. This type of close encounter, with the bear on one side of our window and us on the other, has happened more times than I'm willing to count.

It's a generally accepted rule that bears are not prone to

behave with unprovoked aggression . . . unless they're startled. I think our close proximity to it that night–our noses to the glass looking at it–certainly could've come under that rule. Yet even though the bear was clearly startled by our presence, he did not react by attempting to crash through the window to get at us. Instead, he took the high road and chose to remove himself from the situation. This was encouraging. It was encouraging because there've been numerous incidents in mountain residential communities in which bears have crashed through the glass slider doors of people's decks and patios to ransack kitchen cupboards and refrigerators. That night we considered ourselves lucky–blessed.

Through trial and error we learned that loud noises work best to discourage the bears from visiting our house. So we would rattle the front door (if the bear was already on the porch) or go out another door and shoot a gun into the air.

One morning I was awakened by a terrible rumbly racket on the porch. In that fuzzy state between dream and full consciousness, I initially thought the sound was caused by thunder. Then the visual of the bear filled my mental screen. I raced downstairs and slowly peered out the window behind the computer monitor that looks over the length of the front porch. Sure enough, there was big ole Mr. Black Bear having himself a grand time filling his face with sunflower seeds. He was comfortably sitting on the top log rail and about to stand on it to better scoop the seeds and sweet corn from one of the bird feeders.

I recognized the perfect opportunity to get a good photo of the bear when I saw one. I wanted a shot! I wanted to get a shot of that big bear really bad and, by God, I was going to get me one . . . or two . . . or three or more–as many as I could get!

At this point Sally was on the scene. By the time she grabbed one of the revolvers that we keep handy, I was already sliding the deck door open with fully loaded camera in hand. She told me to give her a sign when I was done getting my shots.

Wincing from the chill of the cold dew on my bare feet, I crept out on our deck, which extended further than the front porch. This gave me a good clear shot of the bear while at the same time keeping me at a safe distance when he eventually saw me. I got three good photos of him, then motioned to Sally. She went out the back door and fired a harmless round into the bank.

The bear took off lickety-split up the drive and . . . sat down to look back at us.

Sally fired the gun again.

The bear cocked his head.

BANG, BANG!

The bear nonchalantly sat there checking his paws for hangnails.

BANG, BANG!

Finally the bear stood up. With one swing of his massive head, he gave us a final disgusted look as if to grumble, "That wasn't very neighborly." Then he ambled off into the woods.

The incident proved interesting. Very interesting, indeed. We felt more like the bear was just plain weary of the noisy game we humans were trying to draw him into and just decided that he didn't want to play anymore. We felt more like it was the bear himself who ended the incident instead of our little noisemaker. We couldn't help but take note that the first time the bear came on the porch the report of the gunshot was enough to chase him off, but the second time, the gun's ear-splitting shot moved him only so far before he sat down to ponder our response to him. We had to wonder if the bear hadn't learned something here. Maybe he realized that the loud noises weren't hurting him in any way. Could the bear be showing a conditioned response? Could a bear differentiate between a noise made to ward him off and a noise that resulted in pain and injury? I don't believe so. But the bear could possibly differentiate the result of a sound associated with a particular *individual.* For example, he might register the difference between our shooting into a bank and *not causing* pain, and a hunter shooting, after *aiming* at the bear, with an intent to *cause* harm.

Also, this bear and probably several more around our property had most likely been aware of us long before they chose to make us aware of them. They had been watching us. Observing us. They had seen us feeding the birds. They had seen raccoons come up on our porch on a nightly basis without being harmed. They had seen seven bucks get so relaxed at twenty paces from the cabin that the two with the largest antlers–the elders with the most experience–actually reclined by the birdbath in the evenings. The bear thinks to himself–well, maybe not actually *thinks* but maybe *senses*–that this is not a place that holds a threat to wildlife. Now don't snicker at that idea or at me for posing it. I'm not so far off the mark with this, because animal behaviorists will readily admit that all animals have learned behavior that comes from experience. Hasn't that been proven with Pavlov's dogs? If the rule of the wild is "survival of the fittest," what makes some more fit than others? The wisdom resulting from learned behavior. Learned knowledge through observation, trial and error and, most important of all, the *remembrance* of those lessons learned in the wild.

So, based on the prickly feeling Sally sometimes gets being watched while out in the deep forest cutting firewood, we'd have to conclude that the bears are tolerating our presence in their own territory. They do not attack, they merely watch. And, likewise, we tolerate their presence near our dwelling without doing them harm.

Though the bears have come onto our porch many times–in early mornings, on bright afternoons, and at night–I think my theory was best borne out on one particularly sunny autumn afternoon. On this balmy day when the scent of woodland spices filled the alpine air, I was sitting indoors at a window seat doing some reading for a book I was working on. A movement outside caught my attention. I was thrilled beyond words to look out and see a mama bear bring her single cub down to the house. You'd have to have been raised on a deserted island not to know how ferociously protective a mother bear is of her cubs. Yet this mother brought her baby down to a place where we humans live! In wonder I watched the two. The mama casually nosed around in the crow bowls filled with dry dog food while the cub strained to reach up, hook its paws around the basin of the birdbath, and comically swing itself back and forth just like a small toddler would be tempted to do. When the fuzzy youngster got bored with that activity, it romped and somersaulted about on the carpet of freshly mown grass.

I ran to get Sally, and we watched the cub lope after its ma while she made her way down the railroad-tie steps running alongside our cabin. The mother bear's bulk swayed as she walked beneath the steep stairway leading up to the porch. When the two were well beyond the steps, we couldn't resist the urge to sneak out on the porch and look down at them. Directly below us, they were an amazing sight.

"Hi, Mama Bear!" Sally had the nerve to greet softly.

Mama looked up and, in the blink of an eye, took off crashing down the slope like an empty raft caught in whitewater rapids. The cub made a weak little grunt and went scampering off behind her.

There's no way that that adult bear couldn't have known there were humans living here. Just no way. Knowing how protective she would've been of her cub, why did this mother chance bringing it so close to us? Was it because she'd previously seen so many varieties of wildlife around us and continually observed that no harm ever came to any of them by our hand? She knew we were here. She felt no threat to herself or her cub because of our presence. Why not? Though she took off like the dickens when she heard Sally's voice and then spotted us above her, her first instinct was *not* to attack us to protect her cub. Her first instinct was to create *distance* between us, even with the cub only ten feet below us. That response spoke volumes. It was telling because the mother bear tore off through the brush leaving her cub in such close proximity to us. Did her instincts carry some assurance that her cub wouldn't be harmed by us? Did her learned sense of us instill trust? It had to have. It had to have, otherwise she'd have turned on us with a vengeance. Something countered that instinct. Something.

We spotted the mother bear and her cub once more that fall. The only other close encounter either of us had (other than those pricklies Sally would still get while out cutting wood) was when I went out after dark one night to refill the feed bowls by the bird feeder that drew in the deer. I was maybe thirty feet from the cabin and had just poured a large scoopful of molasses grain into the first bowl when my hair suddenly stood on end. Then, from down the shadowed slope behind a massive blue spruce, I heard a distinctive sound . . . a loud bear snort. At that, I hightailed it through the garden gate and in the back door as fast as my knee-high mocs could carry me. With my heart pounding like a jackhammer, I raced to the side window.

Nothing. I didn't see a thing move beneath the floodlights that had the entire area lit up like a night baseball game. But my hair doesn't stand on end for nothing.

And I heard what I heard.

A bear was out there.

Sally and I were amazed when we discovered how incredibly quiet bears can be. They can move about like stalking cats. The bears' silent movements don't happen in the woods, of course, where they rustle dry underbrush and snap twigs as they walk by. These huge animals are silent when they are moving about on smooth surfaces like a wooden porch. We've been surprised more than once at night when we have been sitting around reading or watching television and suddenly one of us will be distracted by the movement on the other side of the front picture window . . . right beside us on the porch. It'll be the bear. There have been times when the bear has been on the porch and even the five dogs in the house hadn't heard a thing. Now that's incredible to us.

Once when I was sitting at the computer typing on a manuscript in the middle of a sunny afternoon, I heard a loud thump from the other side of the window behind the monitor. I rose from my chair to peek out, and there was the bear. He'd silently climbed the steps and crossed the length of the porch. He'd lifted the lid on the large wooden feed bin. The thump was the lid banging back against the window frame. Talk about surprised! Both the bear and I jumped because I'd startled him when I called out for Sally to come see.

At the sound of my voice the bear turned tail and lumbered down the steps.

Sally ran for the back door, the bear gun in hand.

The bear stopped at the birdbath.

BANG, BANG!

The bear galloped ten feet further, sat down, and looked back at her.

Instead of firing again, Sally talked to the bear. "I won't hurt you," she calmly said. "We can do this. We can respect each other's spaces. I won't come into your den and you won't come onto my porch. Deal?"

From a window I watched the bear cock his head. This was too weird.

"Deal?" Sally repeated.

As if in reply, the bear stood and gave her a long look, then slowly ambled up the bank and through the aspen stand.

Now I'm not so foolish as to tempt fate, and neither is Sally. I'm also not so arrogant as to think that I'm invulnerable to the wiles of the wilds or that I'm some special nature-loving sprite who emits a magical aura making me impervious to the inherent dangers of life. That'd be a really stupid attitude to have. Yet there is a middle position to take here. For those who choose to live in places carved out of the wild or in remote areas, there is a position of synergistic living.

Mountain living means that humans have breached and invaded the wilds of natural forests, primal woods, and pristine valleys where the multitudes of wildlife species have coexisted for hundreds of years without their habitat being disturbed. They call those forests and valleys home.

Enter the humans. Enter the humans who unthinkingly (or uncaringly) bulldoze burrows and dens, who clear-cut trees housing bird and squirrel, who shatter the serene quietness with a cacophony of noise from their many household machines, who belch smoke into the rarefied air from their coughing vehicle exhausts, and who then think *they're* being invaded when a fox saunters across their drive or a raccoon tips over their trash can. These people don't stop to realize that it was *humanity's* sprawl that encroached upon *nature's* long-established neighborhoods.

Look to the sequence of Creation. The animals came first. Then humans. Then came the human species, who were, supposedly, meant to have the wisdom to be *caregivers* of the animals, not care*takers*–taking away their habitats, their homes, their heartbeats. Having dominion over something does not mean having the power to hold its beating heart in one's hand and, with the arrogance of self-possessed authority, feel one has a divinely granted right to crush or sustain the victim's pulsing life force. Dominion in this case means being respectful of nature by providing wise caregiving and effective management, and recognizing the interdependence of all species. Dominion in this case calls for humans to be the foster parents of the Creatrix's nonhuman life-forms–giving them nurturing, guidance, and protective custody.

All of the separate elements to this bear story are interrelated, and together they exemplify the dynamic Tao of Nature. Tao, a philosophical and spiritual way of living that brings wisdom, peacefulness, and serenity to all who utilize its simplicity.

The Tao of this story clearly relates to Tolerance and Acceptance. The bears have demonstrated a tolerance of the two humans who have moved into their territory. The bears have accepted the fact that we move about their domain and temporarily invade their woods when we gather puffballs, cull out the deadwood from the forests, and take contemplative walks. The bears watch us from a distance when we're out among the pines and firs, and they choose to tolerate our presence.

If a bear can coexist with tolerance for human neighbors, should we be any less tolerant of species differences? Should we be any less accepting of the differences we note? Especially those among the *human* species family? Yet we are, aren't we? Society accepts and tolerates the ideology of Separatism far more readily than it does the Unity of Human Relatedness. This cannot be denied when the evidence strongly underscores that fact.

What evidence? The evidence of people's first response,

knee-jerk reaction to classify everyone they see with an eye that views life through a lens of Separatist Perception. And, sadly, each classification comes weighted with associated personal attitudes.

The fact that our worldwide society of humans has devised so many divisive terms depicts a deplorable state of affairs that should, by now, be way beneath us. As technology advances with intellectual discovery and expanded knowledge, wisdom has lagged far behind. The more intelligent we think we are, the more arrogant we become. Instead of all members of the Human Family pulling together, they nitpick and criticize one another's differences to the point of hating one another. If this weren't so there'd be no crass, denigrating, or vulgar nicknames for people of nationalities that are different from ours.

From religious arrogance to political bickering, the repulsion at ethnic characteristics, and the blindness to lifestyle uniqueness, people see one another through personally designed kaleidoscopes of classifying colors. Diversity, then, is viewed as a negative societal element instead of a wonderful blend of positive facets enriching the whole. We have become accustomed to sifting their sibling human beings through a continually refined Tool of Acceptance called Discrimination. Those not meeting the self-described level of quality are cast aside as being unworthy of our respect or even our time. Taking this analogy further, the perceived human discards are responded to with disgust and negative action is applied against them. The many diverse hate groups that exist around the world thrive on this dissension. It seems that almost everyone has an aversion to someone for whatever reason. Sometimes that reason is the color of someone's skin. Sometimes it's what another believes in. And sometimes it's who another chooses to love or what her occupation is. Sometimes it's as inconsequential as what another is wearing–how he chooses to dress.

Overweight folks shun svelte folks, and thin people cringe and make rude remarks about anyone they determine is too heavy. Christians fear Wiccans and atheists. Republicans are against Democrats. The rich remain aloof from the poor and the middle class. Americans resent and condemn the influx of Hispanics, Asians, and Haitians who are immigrating into their country. Bible-thumpers damn the spiritual freethinkers. The examples are nearly endless.

Why? Why is the list nearly endless?

Why do people love shattering other people's integrity through petty nitpicking? Why do they derive some haughty pleasure in pointing out and making snide remarks about how others differ from themselves? It blows my mind. Where does this hostility toward people's differences–their uniqueness–come from? I don't get it. I don't get why folks wouldn't get more enjoyment from recognizing all the ways in which others are *like* themselves. Or value another's good qualities no matter how different she may appear on the surface. Is it ego that spawns the immediate response of recognizing different qualities rather than like ones? Are humans so insecure that their first response to another is to size him up in an effort to be able to sigh with relief that they themselves are better, taller, smarter, richer, more popular, better dressed, et cetera? Is that it?

If it is then humanity has a lot to learn–a lot to learn from nature, because nature maintains its balance through tolerance of diversity and acceptance of the fact that species need one another. The forests need the ants and termites to break down deadfall and renourish the soil. The botanicals need the bees to cross-pollinate. The land needs the birds to distribute seeds over it. The fish need the algae. People need people. If humans and several bears can manage some relatively workable level of acceptance of each other and find a tolerable common ground, why can't the same be accomplished between human being and human being?

No matter how different someone else is from us, no matter how many kinds of physical characteristics, mannerisms, or beliefs we detect in another, we must not convert these elements into distorted negative or atypical peculiarities to ridicule, shun, nitpick, hate, or denigrate. The proclivity to do so greatly demeans our own character and clearly displays a lack of wisdom and basic sensitivity.

Acceptance is the key.

Tolerance is the padlock that the key opens.

Acceptance of the fact that each one of us is unique and therefore deserves respect is necessary to the enrichment of humanity. The individual qualities each of us has reflect the mirrored intent of a unique soul. We humans are not different species, because we possess varying ethnicities or philosophical beliefs. We are not foreigners if we dress differently. We are not aliens if we belong to a different political party. People are not our enemies if they follow a less-worn path and blaze their own trails through life, if their footfalls keep time to a different rhythm. If we perceive these differentiating characteristics as identification of an enemy to be shunned, ridiculed, or hated, then the true enemy is not the people who carry those qualities. The true enemy lurks not without . . . but within ourselves.

We all share one common family: humanity.

Humanity has just one homeland: earth.

Earth is healthfully sustained by the harmonious interaction of all its many, beautiful species of children.

dancing on diamonds—natural transitions

A WINTER'S TALE.

A tale of stark, raw purity. The purity of nature's annual silent respite in deep hibernation, where the Grand Dreaming of renewal fills the sleepy, hushed hours of each long winter's night, and where the silver twilight brings heightened anticipation of imagined possibilities. Of long awaited-for transitions.

A winter's tale. A tale dispelling the ancient myth and common misunderstanding that winter is a dead season full of lifelessness and bitter winds sweeping over naught but bleak, frosty barrenness. The word *dead* and all of the morbid images it conjures belongs not within the context of this tale for, as you will come to see, the wisdom of the Old Woman of the Woods's wily philosophical ways reaches far, far beyond what can be seen with the naked eye to that which is *knowable* beneath the surface.

Underneath winter's chill there lies an enigmatic warmth, a special kind of blanketed warmth that goes undetected by most of us.

In the spaces between the falling crystals of snowy veils there is a world of little-known magic–a magical truth rarely recognized by humans. An immutable truth that conveys the royal proclamation of winter's high status in the universal nature of things. A high status draped in luminous opalescence and crowned in a dazzling, virginal veil that casts blinding rays from its fragile filaments of diamond dust.

Oh nay! *Nay* I say to the all-consuming wildfire rumors that winter is but a dreary, lifeless span of time! Nay to the faithless, wagging-tongued gossipers who deny winter's inimitable *living* radiance with their begrudging moans and complaints of trudging through a frozen Deadland season! Nay. Oh, nay, I say to them all, for they gravely misinterpret that which they see, and do not perceive that which is open to them.

Oh sweet winter, winter of the Old Woman of the Woods's year coming round full circle, you are the epitome of heartfelt yearning and wide-eyed wonder, of longing hope and deep faith in life's continuum. So pregnant you are with possibilities. So lusciously full of creative imaginings that etch themselves upon the receptive human mind like fairy skate blades leaving their wispy tracks upon a silvery, frozen surface of a hidden woodland pond. Oh winter, within the glorious Cycle of Life, you are the syncopated movement of its ticking clockwork, that sacred metered ticking rarely heard within the human heart.

And so it is that the Old Woman of the Woods's precious season of winter is one of quiet and serene transitions. Seen as such, it's a joyous time of year. Oh, not only because Christmas and other religious holidays happen to come during the winter season but because winter is a time of high celebration all on its own. The garments it wears are royal raiments fit for a queen–the Queen of Winter–who comes bearing unbounded Hope, gestating Renewal, and endless Possibilities that will sprout forth their fertile fruits in springtime.

Haven't you ever just been overwhelmed with awe at the sight of delicate hoarfrost coating pine needles and winter-bare aspen, birch, or maple branches? Been awestruck at how such a visual looks like the frozen-in-time breath left by some great, divine being who passed by during the deep silence of the night? I have.

I've donned a heavy woolen serape and sat in mesmerized wonder out in the winter midnight woods for so long that, when I finally slowly stood and began to move through the pristine, snowy silence, I looked more like a walking snow mound than a human being.

Sequined white glitter covered my hair like sparkling sugar coating, yet I felt no chill from its crystal veil of frozen icing.

White frosting coated my eyelashes like magical mascara applied by a heavenly goddess's pot of diamond dust.

And winking starshine reflected with the ethereal blue moonglow upon the sublimely luminous bejeweled valley, casting a heavenly mercurial light that danced with a rare stellar sense of soul reverie–of high holy sacredness attributed to the blessed essence of the divine, loving Creatrix.

All the while, the evergreen branches, nodding with the sweet breath of the goddess's softly whispered words, acted as swinging incense receptacles that impregnated the hushed surroundings with the fragrant and aromatic spice of forest pine.

Enrapt, I look upward into the spaces that are full. I cannot help but smile while blinking my coated lashes to watch the twirling jewels of perfectly formed symmetrical particles of snow fall as spinning luminaries–fall like crystallized blessings gently being dispersed from the graceful hands of the Divine.

Oh yes, oh winter! So oft has my soul's uncontained joy of it been so bursting with emotion that, upon seeing it snowing I have ignored my shoeless feet and rushed out of the cabin to twirl and dance around in its moonlit magic. Joy! Spinning and twirling with the joy of dancing over diamonds–diamonds dropped from the heavenly cosmos. Pure joy that's so spontaneously unrestrained and expressively uninhibited is a joy unto itself. It's an incredible feeling of emotional abandonment through which pure bliss tickles the soul and makes one infectiously laugh and giggle with the gaiety of a child.

Does this sound like a dead time? Oh, nay 'tis not. 'Tis an enchanting time of sparkling anticipation. 'Tis a season marking the sublime pause in time when a glistening bunting is lovingly wrapped about all of humanity while it rests like a contented infant within its gossamer quilt and contemplates the coming of endless possibilities and dreams of sweet visions of all its gloriously blessed tomorrows.

Wintertime. Winter is nature's season of held breath, the pause during which all the planted seeds–life's wonderful possibilities–gather strength before their birth into the New Beginnings of springtime.

Wintertime can also be seen as a quiet corridor through which one passes from one phase of life to another. Crossing its threshold, one rests within the corridor's quietness, then exits out into the sunlight of new beginnings.

We all have transitions to pass through in life; some folks are presented with more of them than others, but we all meet them along our individual life paths. It's been said that the only sure things in life are death and taxes, but I would add a third–transitions. We all go through them whether we like it or not, whether we want to or not. We can't escape the fact of their existence through our meager attempts to claim denial or ignorance. Some of these transitions are subtle and barely noticed, while others carry intense shock waves and can be emotionally devastating. Some require minor shifts in attitude or acceptance, while others demand major readjustments that involve several facets of one's life.

Most people don't perceive their lives as being full of transitions. Many are of the opinion that their lives are just the same old boring and uneventful routines, day in and day out, but they're wrong. These people are wrong. They see their lives in this way because they don't have the acute awareness of the small changes that are always taking place around them. Or *within* themselves. Our lives are never stagnant pond waters growing foul without the refreshing and rejuvenating current of an underground spring passing through them. Human life has rhythm and meter, and each person's identifiable song is unique and dramatically distinct. Every variation in that metered rhythm represents a new addition or perception a person encounters.

When pointed out, these many variations can be heard and recognized for what they are in our lives–alterations and transitions. The variations of one's life song can be as subtle as a soft ring from one gentle tap on a chime or they can be as disrupting as a reverberating strike on a bass drum. Some influences softly rouse us out of a deep sleep like a loving touch while others cause us to shoot out of bed as though we'd been shouted awake.

So what are these life song variations? What are these alterations to our individualized rhythms? These transitional stages are none other than those simple to sublime events that touch our lives in so many ways. They're the clearly antici–

pated events and unexpected ones that spring out of the shadows along our path. They're the joyful and the sorrowful events. The blessed ones and those we have a tendency to curse. These are all variations to our unique song of life. All transitions that indicate an ending of one life phase and the beginning of another.

It's common to hear about life's larger phases–the "spring" or the "autumn" of one's years, but this isn't what I'm talking about here. The variations of one's life song, the ongoing alteration of one's rhythm I'm speaking of can be felt (and heard) on a daily basis.

It's time to get specific. When one graduates from high school and is cast out into the world to earn a living, that's a variation on one's life song. It represents a stage or phase of transition. When a person falls in love, that's another alteration of her or his formerly very familiar life rhythm. When a love relationship is suddenly shattered, that's one of those booming events that we work through as we face the resulting pain and sorrow. A marriage is another event that causes a vibrational shift in one's life rhythm. A divorce. The news that one is pregnant, and the ultimate birth of that child is another altering variation. Discovering one has a disease. Unexpectedly losing a job because of downsizing or some other political situation within a company. Having to move or relocate to a new area. Receiving a financial windfall. Winning a prestigious award that generates notoriety, such as the Nobel Prize. When we are struck by that sudden spark of clarity that accompanies deep insights about a life problem, our long-held life perspective can be altered in a dramatic way. Epiphanies and profound insights add new notes to the melody of one's life song. An upward-spiraling career that pushes one into the limelight, such as becoming an overnight film star or recording sensation, can also change one's tune. All of these transitions are "winter" seasons that can visit many times in one year.

At one time or another, everyone has probably heard the winter season compared to the darkness of depression or maybe a less severe state of dreariness, grayness, or just the laziness of sitting around and letting the fat cells multiply, as we often do during the physical inactivity of the colder months. Some people see winter as a time of cabin fever that increases anxiety, gives the sense of mental restlessness, creating a feeling of time wasted. But these are only surface perceptions. People see only winter's quilt of snow and not the dynamic import of what lies beneath it. It could be said that the season of winter is, in reality, more fertile than that of springtime. Was that an odd thing to say? Did that seem like a terribly incongruous idea? Again, on the surface, I suppose it could appear that way. Yet when we're within that transitional phase of winter, when some life situation has ended and we're waiting for a new beginning to sprout and show itself, we're suddenly privy to a colorful array of new and undreamed-of options. These options are the seeds waiting for us to recognize and plant. This we do after we have taken time to make choices, after we weigh each seed's unique qualities and choose one to plant in our lives.

Situational endings in life bring us to the point of wintertime. In this season we're given some blessed time of grace to make intellectual, emotional, and spiritual adjustments to those unexpected events that have created an ending. It is the time to come into an acceptance of that ending–a time to rest, reflect, and recognize the fact that most endings are simply doorways to heretofore unthought-of futures. Winter's transition is the time to contemplate this hugely freeing fact. A time of healing when we lick our emotional wounds and gain strength to persevere. A time full of opportunities to learn from hindsight and acquire greater wisdom from analyzing, in an unbiased manner, all the varied elements of the final event that unfolded to reveal itself as an ending. Endings are conclusions. And conclusions open up one's way to new roads and byways that either were not options before or were not perceived as viable possibilities to pursue. This wintertime transitional phase can be a magical dreamtime when old hopes and dreams are again seen beneath the energizing light of possibility. When we look at them this way, many endings in life can be recognized as blessings in disguise.

Blessings in disguise. It sounds trite because the saying has lost its beautiful, vibrantly encouraging meaning with overuse. Yet many times that's just what our lives' situational endings and conclusions turn out to be. Blessings. Blessings that turn our faces to new options and to possibilities that were closed to us before. It's wise never to mentally envision what a specific blessing for oneself will look like or make presumptions about what form it will take, how it will behave or affect our lives. A blessing is just that. It's a gift. It's not the gift's form, or sound, or color that makes it a true blessing, it's how we perceive it as a gift and how we then use wisdom to recognize that precious gift and bring it to its fullest potential.

During this time of winter transition, we ponder what happened, accept that it cannot be altered, and gaze in wonder at all the new doors that've opened before our eyes. Suddenly there is so much to do and think about. So many options! Choices galore. A new and wildly exhilarating sense of freedom and excitement fills the heart with hope. If we allow ourselves to see endings as blessings, we can realize that each one gives us a second chance. With each one we are reborn!

The wintertime phases of transition following endings are wonderful opportunities to better ourselves, improve our relationships, and adjust to destiny's new directions. Winter is a corrective period. A corrective period in which we can gain valuable insights and experiential wisdom.

But what of the ultimate ending? What of death? Don't folks often refer to those who are elderly and very sick as being in the "winter of their years"? Don't people equate the season of winter with the ending of one's allotted time here in the physical world? Sure they do. You've heard it as often as I have. Yet why is that? Why, I wonder. Especially when we've just seen how beautifully encouraging the time between endings and new beginnings can be in other life situations. What makes a physical death any different? What makes the *final,* ultimate ending any different than all the others that came before it? A transition is a transition. An ending makes way for a new beginning. We are made up of energy–spirit energy–and that energy is just changing its attire when our physical human form dies. Like a snake sloughing off its old skin, like a butterfly being freed from its cocoon, the spirit moves into the wintertime transitional phase upon the demise of its physical shell casing. And if you thought that a situational life ending opened up a grand vista of new possibilities for the *living* individual, think what the freed *spirit* might be presented with. Why, the potential is mind-boggling! Joy. Pure freedom. Knowledge. Choices beyond imagining!

The wintertime transitional stage following human physical death is the adjustment phase of the spirit between lifetimes or destinies, for not every spirit that is newly passed-over requires another reincarnational experience. For those who do, this stage is one of learning from past mistakes made while in the physical form; it involves gaining wisdom and making new choices for rebirth–a springtime phase in the physical. Physical death of the human body is merely a transition for one's spirit into a finer vibrational frequency. The physical death is but a moving on, an ending that precedes the ultimate new beginning where the doors to possibilities are endless and beyond anyone's human comprehension.

We can't grasp the infinite possibilities the spirit is presented with when it passes beyond its physical ending because the human mind is so limited in its visionary imaginings. The human mind is so minute in its capacity for total understanding. We humans can't even envision the actual scope of our universe, or that there may be more than one universe. How, then, can we begin to imagine the shimmering and spectacularly infinite possibilities available to the newly passed spirit? What we have to choose from at that time is awesome. Simply awesome. There is no other word for it. There is no other word to describe the ways and means that a spirit can opportune itself with new beginnings. A spirit's wintertime transitional phase is full of pure beauty, unconditional love, potential, and new knowledge. For a spirit, the winter phase is one of great expectations for itself. At this stage the spirit is brimming with excitement as it gleans personal wisdom from past mistakes made while in the physical and looks ahead with anticipation to a new beginning wherever it decides would best suit its unique purpose and destiny.

Oh no, death is not the frigid barrenness of a colorless winter. Death is the glorious transition from an ending into a bright and sunny new day. A dawning day full of life. A day full of joy and exciting plans. A beginning day that can only be classified as the Quintessential New Beginning–one full of sparkling diamonds that are seen as glittering, priceless possibilities to be dazzled by, to tightly embrace and, ultimately, to dance upon.

punkin pie—loyalty

SALLY AND I CURRENTLY HAVE A TEN-MONTH-old husky pup I named Una and four older Yorkshire terriers who share our cabin homestead. We started out with the one Yorkie named Baby that belonged to Sally. This Yorkie was very pregnant when they both came to live with me. Baby's first litter produced three males and one female. The female was very small, so small that some would call her the runt of the litter. Sally gifted this tenacious little runt, who was as cute as a button, to me and I named her Pinecone because she wasn't any bigger than one.

My little Pinecone ended up being completely silver, just like her daddy, and at six years of age, she still weighs only three pounds. Her active legs are no thicker than some of the stick kindling I gather during the autumn and just as fragile as those twigs. As soon as she was weaned, Pinecone attached herself to me. She would curl up in my lap while I sat and read in the evenings or while I worked on a new manuscript. If I sat at the computer, she was right there, nestled in the folds of my skirt. When bedtime rolled around, she had a favorite place to snuggle in beside me. If I reclined on my side on the couch, she'd immediately jump up on my waist and make that her resting perch. Pinecone is one very special little Yorkie who continues to amaze people with her small size and huge black eyes shining out from the high contrast of her silvery face. Some people have commented that she looks like a little ghost. Pinecone is one of a kind. But then I suppose all dog owners could be heard saying the same thing about their little canine "babies."

Some months after the birth of Pinecone, Sally took Baby to a friend's house where Pinecone's daddy lived. Sally wasn't in the door five minutes when Baby and Buddy were "in serious throes of love" again! Inevitably, Baby grew to look like a melon waddling around on short, furry legs. This time she produced one male and two females. Our friend's son took the male pup and named him Badger. Baby's other two pups were so cute and we'd gotten so attached to them that, well, we just couldn't part with the new additions and we now had four Yorkies! Sally named one new puppy Rosebud, and I named the other one Punkin Pie. Rosie was gregarious, smart as a fox, and full of vinegar. Punkin Pie's smarts seemed to be a few Milk-Bones short of a full box, and her name ended up fitting her to a T. Right from the beginning, her attachment to me surpassed that of her big sister, Pinecone. Yet Pinecone was never displaced by Pie. There was room around me for them both. Fortunately, neither one showed any jealousy or possessiveness.

Punkin would follow on my heels all through the house. She'd keep her eyes on me when we were in the same room—which was almost always. If I went into the bathroom and was rude enough to close the door behind me, she'd scratch on it until I let her in. Pie sits right beside me on the couch and curls up beneath my office chair whenever I'm working at the computer. She'll stay there for hours. As long as I'm typing, she's perfectly content to be sleeping at my feet. When I get up she follows me. And when I walk into a room, she keenly watches to see where I'm going to sit before she decides where she's going to settle down. If someone other than myself gives her a command, she'll look to me for confirmation before she obeys. When something frightens her, she beelines it through the cabin and takes a flying leap onto my lap for protection. And one winter when I contracted the flu and took to my bed for two days, Pie kept my feet warm and refused to leave the room.

Punkin Pie has an extraordinary ability to convey her feelings. She has a special posture that just exudes the love she feels for me. She'll sit with her body leaning forward, her tail wagging, and her eyes riveted to mine, as if using all of her canine might of communication to convey "I love you. The sun sets and the moon rises on you and you alone." I'm sure other dog owners have seen this behavior in their furry friends' eyes too. And when I have to leave the house, Punkin Pie pouts, yet when I return all is instantly forgiven and I'm inundated with Pie's ecstatic greetings, which won't quiet until I pick her up and accept her insistent kisses.

Baby responds the same way with Sally. She adores her.

Ahh, to live with the freely expressed demonstrations of such pure emotion is a real heart-welling joy. A blessing, a true blessing from above. To know that a little being misses you when you're gone and is so incredibly happy upon your return is awesomely heartwarming. To have a loving dog snuggle beside you in the evenings and instill deep feelings of perfect contentment in you is a type of comfort that cannot be adequately named or clearly defined. This unconditional love, this unconditional loyalty soothes one's heart and warms one's soul.

Loyalty.

Loyalty is what this little Punkin Pie has filled her glowing aura with. And though much of her body language also speaks clearly of a deeply affectionate adoration, the two must never be perceived as being the same when applied to human loyalty. Only in the latter context must the two never, ever be perceived as synonymous in nature and intent. Human loyalty will not tolerate attendant adoration. Loyalty must always stand alone. It must always stand without being supported or weighted down by extraneous emotions that diminish its shining beauty. Loyalty must forever stand on its own. And it does.

For me, Punkin Pie has been the quintessential example of the free expression of unconditional loyalty and faithfulness, yet I've also observed other examples in nature. Birds and animals who are known to mate for life exhibit this kind of loyalty, which involves a commitment of self to another and communicates an unspoken vow of fidelity and trust. This loyalty is pure and free from extraneous agendas. It's unadulterated and magnificently beautiful in its simplicity.

The same cannot always be said about the inherent quality of *human* loyalty though. Often human loyalty is tainted. Its pollutants are those insipid, self-serving motives hidden from view. They're as insidious and treacherous as the most dangerous virus. These are an individual's secret agendas, which become attached to the underside of loyalty's sleek keel. They are the encrusted barnacles that cause quickly multiplying encumbrances. Ultimately, one's original loyalty becomes so burdened that it's smothered. So thoroughly weighted down with these hidden intentions, the Ship of Loyalty eventually sinks under its own load of misshapen agendas.

Many times people don't even realize that they've attached personal and negative qualities to their loyalty because these motivations develop quite silently and germinate out of the many minuscule seeds representing one's goals and desires. These harmful seeds of agenda sprout from one's ego, one's ultimate focus on self. This focus introduces a contradiction in terms and intent. Displaying loyalty to another while qualifying that loyalty with thoughts of oneself is like mixing oil and water. One's show of loyalty should never be energized by intentions of getting something in return. Nor should one's loyalty be deepened by thoughts of self. For then loyalty is nothing more than a scam of insincerity.

If loyalty is to remain pure and simple, it must be just that–pure and simple. It must not be exhibited to puff yourself up by being able to proclaim that you rub shoulders with someone famous, or to get yourself into a prestigious inner circle, or to raise yourself another rung on the social ladder or another level in your line of business. Ingratiating yourself in the guise of loyalty is a hard blow to your character that is seldom seen coming and is even more seldom felt, because a person with such thoughts has a mind so focused on gaining *personal* ground that the *means* of doing so is rationalized into total acceptability.

Loyalty is one of those attributes that casts a broad net over the waters of society. It encompasses many aspects of our lives because, as human beings, we have very specific thoughts on everything under the sun, from who our favorite presidential candidate is to what we believe about God and the right way to express that belief. Political affiliations, religious beliefs, ethics, and morals are all affected by the loyalty people feel and show toward them. Whether we hold a strong sense of obligation toward saving the rain forests or fighting some type of social discrimination, we all have causes that we can be passionate about. One's family, a philosophical concept, a scientific theory, a friend, a favorite author, a life goal or career aspiration, all represent valid objects to which people direct their loyalties. Most often when they hear the word *loyalty,* people associate the term and all it entails with a person, with human relationships, yet we see that the attribute of loyalty actually touches a multitude of elements in one's life.

Loyalty cannot exist without belief. A strong belief in another individual, a religious dogma, a political party, a philosophical concept, a scientific theory, is the sole impetus behind a growing sense of loyalty. This fact isn't something folks usually give much thought to. Loyalty evolves out of belief. If that belief is strong, so is the depth of loyalty shown. If the belief begins to wane or is shaken for one reason or another, the level of loyalty quickly follows suit. It weakens. As Above, so Below. When the mind (intellect) begins to doubt a formerly held belief, the heart (emotions) lessens in kind.

Conviction, meaning the intensity of its fervor, can either magnify one's loyalty to an impassioned zealousness or reduce it to ashes that are blown away by the slightest breeze of doubt. This fact is repeatedly proven on the nightly newscasts. A group of animated protesters converge on the steps of a city hall to proclaim their opinion to the attracted bystanders. The ardent protesters are moved to action by deep loyalty to their specific belief, while the quiet bystanders feel no such passion. A strong belief can spur vehement loyalty, while a weak or undecided belief will leave loyalty lacking. Therefore, a show of loyalty is nothing more substantial than a paper mask if there is no conviction to support it. Loyalty without the integrity of conviction is a disguise some wear with experienced aplomb.

They wear it without guilt of conscience because they think it serves their egos well.

This leads us to yet another element of human behavior–integrity. Loyalty must carry a full complement of integrity if it is to be a pure and unencumbered quality. It may be surprising, that integrity is best demonstrated when addressing loyalty to oneself. Another way to convey this idea is through the concept of being true to oneself. We've heard this phrase over and over again, yet how many times have we actually taken the time to stop and contemplate what it means? It certainly doesn't mean that we must love and stroke our egos. Neither does it imply that we must place ourselves above the crowd. And it definitely doesn't mean for us always to put our own motives at the top of the list. It has nothing to do with prioritizing ourselves. It has everything to do with making sure that our relationships and loyalties, our actions and reactions, are not loaded down with extraneous, self-serving attitudes and ulterior motivations.

Integrity not only means being honest about one's loyalties but also means that, first and foremost, one is honest with oneself–completely. When we are examining our loyalties, if any form of self-serving motivation is found lurking in the dark corners, those loyalties are severely compromising the quality of one's personal integrity.

So what does "being true to oneself" mean? The fundamental meaning is that a person is absolutely loyal to his or her personally held philosophies, ethics, spiritual beliefs, and behavioral traits. It means that one doesn't shrink away from opportunities to express alternative ideas in the face of a differing popular opinion. It means that a person isn't coerced into agreeing to something she or he doesn't believe in simply to avoid ridicule or verbal confrontation. It means that an individual is never embarrassed by his or her convictions, no matter how unusual or unconventional they may appear. Personal integrity comes from being loyal to oneself and never denying one's beliefs.

Personal integrity shines brightest when we refuse to let the ego invade our behavior, convictions, and loyalties. It's doing for others just because you believe that it's the right thing to do–doing for others without any strings attached, without any thought to what you might get out of it for yourself . . . even if that's something as subtle as wanting to be recognized as a person who is always ready to assist others. That would be an example of conditional goodness, and we never want to slip into action spurred by such a self-serving motivation. Frequently people don't even realize that they're offering help to others all the time for the underlying purpose of wanting to be liked and appreciated. Of course there are many, many folks who just love helping others without having any type of self-serving strings attached to the ego. These people just plain enjoy helping others, that's part of who they are, part of their innate personality, and that's being true to self. That's having pure, unadulterated integrity.

Without personal integrity, without routinely being true to one's own philosophies and convictions, one's entire life is not grounded, is not lived with feet planted firmly on the ground. Indeed, an individual such as this will never, ever truly know his or her own self.

So many times I've observed people behave in a manner that is based on the opinion of others. These folks say what those around them want to hear. They'll agree with concepts or opinions that are contrary to their own convictions so others will count them as part of the crowd. Afraid of being ostracized, these people agree with whatever the group opinion is. This is not personal integrity. So what if your opinion or perspective differs? So what if you openly express that differing opinion or belief and receive sidelong looks or snide comments? So what? The mind's consciousness is unique to each individual. Not everyone holds firm to the same beliefs. Not everyone is passionate about the same issues. Not everyone believes in a Divine Being living up in someplace called Heaven. Our philosophical differences are what make each of us so uniquely beautiful! Magnificently diverse and brilliantly colorful! Intentionally hiding that uniqueness beneath a suffocating gray shroud of conformity is not being loyal to oneself.

Now I will admit to holding opinions different from those shared by a group of people I'm with and not airing my point of view in order to avoid a confrontation that I know will go nowhere and solve nothing. But I have never compromised my integrity by *agreeing* with that group's opposing opinion. Sometimes silence is as golden as they say it is–maybe even more so. Keeping silent can preserve one's integrity. Keeping silent is, more times than one might think, an act of quiet wisdom. Sometimes keeping silent can convey more than any words can. Indeed, keeping silent can be a means of exuding power that is dramatically felt by others. Not that that was your specific intent, that's just the natural effect silence can have.

So the next time you find yourself involved in a conversation in which you appear to be the only one holding a differing opinion, instead of compromising your integrity, try not saying anything. You can joke and tell the group that you're sitting this one out, that *observing* a conversation is sometimes more revealing than *participating* in it. Just don't cave in on your integrity and agree with a concept or opinion that you really, in your heart and mind, strongly oppose just for the sake of being accepted. Stay true to yourself. Keep your integrity intact. Be loyal to your own beliefs and opinions. Don't betray them for the sake of others or for the purpose of being accepted. To do those things is to betray yourself.

Few people look at loyalty in this light. They don't think much about what being loyal to themselves entails. Now I know that it's natural to want to be liked and accepted by others. But when one's own integrity is sacrificed, who is it that these others are liking and accepting? Isn't this "who" a false individual if her or his integrity has been bartered in the name of popularity? And does this individual eventually lose sight of their identity? In the end the person doesn't even know himself or herself anymore because so much of that self (beliefs, perceptions, attitudes) has been swayed to others in order to be counted as one of the crowd.

One of the crowd. A clique. The "group." The inner circle. Yuck! Incredibly stomach-turning! Gross! It's all of those gaggy things if one has exchanged integrity for it. It's also extremely sad. It's sad not to want to be oneself. It's a pitiful thing to give up one's integrity for loyalty to others, or to a cause one doesn't believe in, or just to stroke the ego by wanting so much to be accepted or liked. Oh yes, that's incredibly sad.

Giving up one's integrity for the sake of showing false loyalty drowns one's uniqueness in a quagmire of conformity. It smothers one's loyalty to self under a heavy, wet blanket of self-destruction. It kills one's self-esteem. Then such a person wonders why he or she is depressed. Why life has lost its sparkle, its meaning. Well, hello! That individual had traded all she or he held dear for acceptance by others! That individual doesn't even know who she or he is anymore. There's a little secret to life that few give serious thought to: *Your integrity is the framework of the Who of you.* It's your unique identity. It's what gives you that wonderfully ecstatic feeling of being blessed with a basketful of grace when you perform an act of unconditional goodness. It's what subtly and sometimes not so subtly enhances one's self-esteem. It gifts one with an unasked-for sense of greater self-worth—one that conveys the comforting awareness that one is making a difference in the lives of those around one. It encourages and enriches one's sense of purpose.

Right about now I can hear some of you readers mumbling something like this: "Oh, right. Staying true to oneself does all this?"

You bet your sweet dreams it does. It does all that and more–so much more. The benefits of maintaining one's integrity and staying loyal to oneself are countless. If you take more than a bit of time to think about it, *really* analyze the concept and deeply contemplate on it, you'll see what I'm talking about here. I'm trying to stress the importance of staying loyal to oneself. I'm striving to bring home the point that, unless you're true to all you personally believe in, you can never look your mirrored reflection in the eye and feel confident about being completely honest and living a life that shines with your beautiful individuality. You will never feel that wonderful sense of being loyal to your own core beingness. And that, my friends, is a priceless blessing that only you can ensure. One that only you can bring to yourself as a personal gift of self-worth to bathe in luxuriously without one twinge of guilt.

Integrity is not a negative attachment to ego. Quite conversely, integrity is vital to maintaining the true, innate beingness of the essential self. It is the very *preservation* of one's basic and pure nature, one's unique personality, one's unparalleled set of innate qualities that, all combined, make each of us who and what we are. So my question would be: Why on earth would anyone wish to distort, encumber, or shatter these glorious qualities of individual beingness by behaving in a manner other than the one that engenders complete loyalty to oneself?

By straying from such behavior, a person quickly becomes nothing more than a stranger to self. A stranger who no longer knows her or his own mind. A stranger who loses mental focus on long-held goals and is thrown into psychological, intellectual, and spiritual confusion. These are surefire eventualities because, forsaking loyalty to one's beliefs, ethics, and opinions, one loses sight of self and suffers nothing less than the death of identity. Self-esteem plummets. Such a person finds himself or herself in the throes of more frequent bouts of anger or rage that he or she cannot trace to a specific source. Rage at the world boils up and spills over to affect those around this person. Depression, a boundless black void, can be a frequent visitor.

These side effects of losing one's integrity are real–all too real. Psychiatrists' waiting rooms are full of people who feel lost, displaced in life. They lost their loyalty to self as they tried to fill a desperate need to be liked and accepted by others. Morgues have seen their share of the lifeless shells that are all that remain of some of these folks. Yes, the loss of self can be as serious as that. Not recognizing the importance of one's integrity can be a fatal mistake. Those who lose a sense of self cast off their personal identity in favor of an unfamiliar cloak of a complete stranger–a stranger who is more acceptable and appealing to others. But one may come to despise this false identity. By then it may be too late to shed it.

What about loyalty to others?

Loyalty to others is a bit different from loyalty to oneself (and the integrity associated with it). At the outset I want to state an incontrovertible fact: *Loyalty to others should never be blind.* Loyalty to others must be given with both eyes open–wide open. It must be constantly monitored with reason and logic. We must keep a close eye on the people to whom we entrust our loyalty. Loyalty given to someone whose integrity is slipping away is not well-placed. This is what is meant by the fact that loyalty must never be blind. Knowledge is the keeper of one's loyalty gauge. So is awareness.

For example, if one is loyal to a group devoted to a specific cause, that loyalty can be considered well placed until one becomes aware of that group's subtle shifts to acts of violence or other types of negative behavior. Such knowledge should never be ignored simply for the sake of maintaining loyalty. The changing behavior of that group becomes a devotee's personal responsibility to spend time reassessing. Maybe loyalty should no longer be pledged to their cause.

If a religious dogma one strongly believes in is suddenly shaken in the light of expanded research, one compromises one's integrity by remaining loyal to that dogma. Knowledge often alters loyalty when one makes personal integrity the top priority in life.

When a person is adamantly loyal to a certain individual who goes on to do something unconscionable, that once loyal person should not be blind. He or she should not ignore grave ethical or spiritual transgressions. Loyalty is earned. And it's usually earned through proof of integrity.

How many times have we witnessed the fall of role models in society? Most of us can name at least one sports figure whose fans were staunchly loyal until unacceptable behavior–usually some lack of sportsmanship or the exposure of a crime–shattered their devotion. The formerly loyal fan is plunged into a state of shock, but this shock is a sign of the fan's integrity. It shows that his or her loyalty is not given blindly. No matter how strong the loyalty, it can be retracted if integrity slips. That's the way loyalty must be given–there must be an expectation of integrity.

We all know that there's not a single person walking this planet who can be said to be without some fault, to be perfect. If we were perfect we wouldn't be here on earth; the fact that people have faults and flaws is accepted by almost everyone. We all make mistakes, err on the side of bad judgment, make irrational decisions, and catch ourselves displaying ill-mannered behavior or regrettable knee-jerk reactions. But these kinds of slips don't make us bad people–they don't usually shake the loyalty of our friends and family. Loyalty that is given with integrity and reason in mind allows for human frailty. We wouldn't think of removing our loyalty to a family member who made an error or two in good judgment, or a friend who made a bad decision. These mini-goofs are not what we're talking about here. We're talking about seriously grave negative behaviors that send shock waves through the very ground on which a loyal individual stands.

Intellectual reason and rationality are loyalty's permanent housemates. To say that *wisdom* is a prime member of that House of Loyalty would be a gross understatement. In fact wisdom is the very foundation of that house. These important elements of loyalty are what keep personal integrity on its toes and maintain its purity of form and substance.

One of the last yet essential aspects to include in conveying the importance of personal integrity as it's related to loyalty is that *"obligation" should never compromise the reasons for one's loyalty.* Loyalty is never obligatory. Remember, it has no strings attached. No ulterior motives. Carries no sense of guilt if not openly demonstrated. Otherwise it's tainted by psychological negatives that make it, something it was never intended to be.

What are these psychological negatives? Well, let's stay with the idea of obligation. Sometimes loyalty to another has been well-deserved; sometimes it's been well-deserved for a long while. But then something happens that prompts the loyal individual to question that long-held allegiance. The individual begins to feel uncomfortable showing or expressing loyalty as strongly as she or he has in the past. Maybe this person has spent long hours attempting to pinpoint the source of the newfound doubt. All this formerly faithful person knows for sure is that the level of dedication to the other individual has diminished. Something's shifted. He or she no longer feels the loyalty as steadfastly as before.

Unsuspecting individuals can find themselves drawn toward fidelity. We might even say they're caught fast in an invisible net of obligation caused by long-term loyalty that is difficult to abandon or break. But a person in this situation must find a way to extricate himself or herself from it, because once loyalty has lost its conviction in a solid sense of belief, the loyal individual will lose self-worth. When belief in a person, group, or idea wanes, loyalty can no longer be given. If a person continues to be faithful in spite of doubts, he or she will suffer. Once an obligation to maintain loyalty enters the picture, the entire relationship becomes distorted with doubts and misshapen with a prevailing attitude of self-deprecation. These come as direct results of not being true to oneself.

So, if an allegiance has waned for some reason, why keep up the facade? What or who does that behavior serve? Isn't a false front the same thing as insincerity? Therefore, how can insincerity (blatantly displayed or subtly sequestered, recognized or denied) possibly–even remotely–serve the recipient of a once staunchly honest, supportive attitude? I think most of us would agree that no person and no cause can be served by a pretense of solidarity. No one wants unwilling supporters lining up beside her or him. I don't believe anyone would want to hear double-talk or lip service from patrons or associates. And nobody wants to be surrounded by reluctant participants who have lost the driving passion that once kept them focused on their loyalty.

When a sense of loyalty wanes, what prevents a person from being straightforward about the lessened feeling? What reinforces false loyalty? Most of the causes for this situation are tightly woven into the fabric of the individual's psychological makeup and are directly associated with ego–the sense of self is fearful of being humiliated, demeaned, or ridiculed by an accusation of disloyalty. Because of these fears, the individual continues to express loyalty with false sincerity because he or she has a personal agenda to maintain the status of his or her ego. This ends up being a loyalty perpetrated to protect one's image. Such outwardly expressed loyalty lacks true resolve toward the recipient or cause and instead becomes solely motivated by selfishness.

Many times this situation causes unrest within a person, yet the discomfort it creates is overidden by a desire to preserve personal image as perceived by the public at large. The inner conflict simmers on the back burner of consciousness. The person's ego desires respect for self, yet this person still has an underlying knowledge that the respect others demonstrate toward him or her isn't quite deserved.

Ohh, what messes we get ourselves into when the ego is stronger than our sense of integrity. What self-destructive psychological webs we weave when we sidestep honesty with others and, most important, with ourselves. How warped our reflections become when we gaze into them. Yet these distorted images are only seen and acknowledged if we have consciences. Without that all-important, self-regulating conscience, personal integrity and self-esteem can be continually and quite easily manipulated by whichever devious manners and prevaricative means we see fit to employ. No twinges of guilt can penetrate the conscience once intellectual rationalizations toughen the skin of self-respect into shoe leather. These mind games are most often created for a player of one–oneself. There are countless ways people can manipulate themselves with self-soothing rationales and twisted logic that, on the surface, make bad behavior an acceptable act.

Like that of my little Punkin Pie, true loyalty comes from a heart unburdened by the ugly encumbrances of obligation. It comes from a heart uncluttered by personal motives and additional agendas. The loyalty has not been coerced or even asked for. It grows out of genuine love and commitment to another. It is untainted . . . pure. Just as ours should be and forever remain if we expect to keep our integrity intact and hold it high as a precious gift of gold–a shining divine blessing–to cherish and protect behind the powerful shield of a clear conscience.

coyote at play—balance of reality

MANY YEARS AGO, AT A TIME THAT NOW SEEMS like some foggy other lifetime, I lived in a small cabin with my marriage partner, Bill. Our three beautiful daughters were grown, out of the family nest, and on their own by then. We two were left to work on making a success of a twenty-six-year relationship that appeared to be unraveling.

On one of those brilliant and clear autumn afternoons when rays of golden light speared down through the pine branches like delicate, divine fingers, I was standing at the kitchen window waiting for the angel-hair pasta to finish cooking. Never missing an opportunity to feel blessed for living in the mountains, I was taking advantage of this waiting period to feast my eyes on the stand of pine trees that surrounded the place. Lowering my gaze to the natural groupings of granite rocks spread at the bases of the wide old ponderosa trunks, I was gifted with the sight of a little chipmunk sitting up on her haunches. She was looking back at me. A smile of amusement came to my face when I noticed how her cheek pouches bulged like twin gunnysacks filled with tightly packed seeds.

"Well, hello, little lady," I whispered through the screen. "How are you on this fine afternoon? I see you've been busy gathering food for your family! What a good little provider you are!" And, not two seconds later, a feral cat sprang like a bolt of lightning out of nowhere and sprinted off with the little mother squirming in its mouth.

To say I was startled would be an understatement. My stomach turned inside out, and my heart lunged against my rib cage. Tears welled in my eyes. "Oh, *God*!" I exclaimed as I crossed my hands over my chest. "Oh, my *God*!"

From the living room, Bill asked what was wrong.

I was so stunned that I could hardly get the words out. "A feral cat . . . a feral house cat just came out of *nowhere* and . . . and ran off with the little chipper I was talking to! Ohh, God, it was so . . . it was so *sickening* to see that!"

Without a half ounce of sympathy for my feelings or a quarter ounce of empathy for the little critter that'd just lost its sweet life, my partner snapped back, "Well, Ms. Nature Nymph, put *that* in your books!"

My shock was intensified. "What do you mean?" I asked.

He sarcastically chuckled. "You write about nature's sweetness and light so much that people are getting sick of hearing about it. You're always going on and on ad nauseam about nature's *beautiful* this, its *heart-lifting* that, but you never write about the dark side. You never write about the *reality* of its viciousness or its deadly nature, do you? Why the hell not?

What's the matter, you in denial over that side of it? Would you rather *pretend* it didn't exist?"

His words stung.

"No," I quickly responded, "I'm not in denial of nature's reality. I don't bother writing about the darker elements because everyone already *knows* nature is balanced by daily deaths in the wild. I'm trying to lift people up and open their eyes to nature's beauty and how it can be an effective *asset* in their lives if they'd just give it some *notice* and let it *comfort* them. Writing about the darker side wouldn't accomplish that goal."

"That's a bunch of bullshit," he snickered back. "What a crock. You're in denial."

My heart was still aching for the little furry chipmunk who'd been taken as off guard as I'd been by the silent swiftness of the cat. I wasn't in the mood to escalate this discussion into a full-blown argument with Bill. Instead, I fell silent and remained that way. This voluntary choice of silence cut off the issue, even though my gloating partner thought it'd ended with him getting the best of me. I didn't care about that. I never needed to have the last word or end up with the upper hand. Instead, I wiped at my eyes and returned to preparing supper. Although there were two bodies occupying our bed that night, their hearts and minds couldn't have been drifting further apart.

As I said at the beginning, that incident happened many years ago, but it's relevant to this nature tale. Now I live in a different cabin, situated on ten acres, with someone else—someone I care deeply for, someone who loves nature, the forests, and all the critters living in them just about as much as I do.

The "business" section of this cabin's office area is confined within an eight-by-eight-foot room that is graced with three windows and two skylights. These give me the sense of working outside . . . well, almost. One window looks beyond the computer monitor onto the covered front porch, which is constantly aflutter with many species of feeding birds. The window to my left provides a peaceful view of the mountain valley, which gently slopes down from the front of the cabin, and the one behind me is partly obscured by an old oak rolltop desk.

To some folks this work space may seem cramped, yet I can work at the computer and, with just a half swivel of the chair, be facing my desk, where reference books and file drawers are within arm's reach. It's not cramped at all, it's the epitome of efficiency and convenience. Most of all, because of all those marvelous windows, this workplace is the quintessential source of inspiration for a nature-loving writer such as myself. It's those glorious windows always presenting ever-changing scenes that heighten my joy and expand my inspiration. I'll be the first to admit that this space is actually more of an observation room, which will sometimes distract me more from my work than contribute to my productivity.

While working on a manuscript, I'll suddenly spot a new species of bird that's come to feed at one of the porch feeders and, having no compunction to remain focused on the book, I'll leave what I'm doing to rush into the living room and sit on the cedar chest below the picture window to watch the newcomer for a while. Or I'll suddenly be quite surprised to discover that a black bear has surreptitiously climbed the porch steps to help herself to the wealth of sunflower seeds and molasses-flavored sweet feed that sits there. Or unusual cloud formations will draw my attention. Or a spectacular, fire-in-the-sky sunset that floods the office room with a warm amber glow will send me racing out onto the porch to stand in wonder over nature's splendor.

Oh yes. Yes! The hundreds of working hours spent in this

office are abundantly sprinkled with nature's tantalizing spices and provocative sensory seasonings, which never fail to entice my ever–hungry soul. Ahh, well, being who I am; that is, *how* I am–knowing how sensitive and responsive I am to nature and all its prodigious attributes, I wouldn't have it any other way now, would I? I count these daily sightings as extraordinary blessings that cause my heart to well up, and these little joys far outweigh the inconvenience of frequently having my work interrupted. They serve as a powerful impetus to work harder and give me the energy boost to do just that once I return to the keyboard with a greatly appreciated sense of renewed vigor.

One such joy visited in the middle of winter, when I was intently writing *Beyond Earthway.* It was a cold, crisp high alpine day, and the dazzling sunshine made the heavy blanket of snow sparkle as though it was woven of pure spun silver. The logs in the living room woodstove were crackling and snap–ping. A scratching on the cedar siding beside the window to my left took my attention away from the computer monitor. I turned to see our little squirrel clinging to the wood and curi–ously peering in at me.

"Hello, little fella!" I greeted.

He flicked his bushy tail a couple of times and scampered to the other side of the window to get a better view. He looked down at the table full of papers and, I guess, since there wasn't anything interesting there, like acorns or sunflower seeds, he quickly scurried around to the porch, where the feeders were full of goodies.

My sights didn't switch to the window behind the moni–tor, where I would've seen him eating. My attention remained at the side window where the squirrel had first appeared for, beyond the pine tree, I saw a lone coyote romping in the snowy valley below. Amused, I rested back in the chair to watch this solitary playacting.

Jumping and leaping high.

Pouncing and jumping back.

Burying its nose and running to and fro.

Oh, this coyote was having the grandest time of his life playing down there in the deep snowy powder. His joyous antics brought a wide smile to my face until . . . I noticed that he wasn't playing alone.

He had a playmate that he was tossing up in the air.

My smile vanished quicker than a mime's.

The coyote was toying with its tiny prey.

My smile turned down into a frown of sadness.

And, reverberating through the forgotten, cobwebbed corridors of my mind, I heard an unwelcome echo from the past ring out, "Well, Ms. Nature Nymph, put *that* in your books!"

It had been many years since I'd heard that comment from Bill, yet during all those years I'd grown through the personal experience and gentle wisdom I'd drawn from spending much more time observing nature. Those observations have served to mature my thought processes and mellow my once-rash perspectives and responses. Some of my impetuousness has evolved into patience, and most of my anxiety has transformed into acceptance. I believe I've gained a true perception of reality as it maintains its fine and precarious balance of precisely placed counterweights.

A glass cannot be half full unless it is also half empty. If a psychologist places such a glass before you and asks you what you see, the right answer is *supposed* to be: "A glass that's half *full.*" That's supposed to show a tendency toward optimism rather than pessimism or depression. Yet I would disagree with that alleged right answer because it's incomplete. It's unbalanced. Why does one's attitude have to be outweighed by optimism rather than *balanced* with a perception of actual reality, of seeing the glass as *both* half full and half empty? To my way of thinking, the right answer is to see it both ways instead.

And so the passing of the years has expanded my perception of life's true reality and its balance. Though seeing that playful coyote down in the valley brought a smile to my face, it also brought a frown when thoughts turned to the tiny prey being tossed about in the air like a Frisbee.

Balance.

The balance of life is never exhibited in such an exacting and pure form as it is in nature. Nature is unbiased. It has no personalized affectations such as the ego or individual agendas. Life is instinctual–natural. The Grand Balance to Nature is that it is both half full and half empty.

It was because of this truth that I continued to watch the coyote at play instead of turning aside with disgust. I didn't jump to the negative perspective and become sickened by perceiving him as a vicious killer. To the contrary, I saw what he was doing and still perceived his beauty. His coat was thick and full, his tail was long and bushy. Clearly, his energy level was high enough to savor some playtime before getting down to the more serious business of satisfying his hunger.

From the distance between us, I couldn't positively identify what the coyote's meal was going to be. It was some little critter he'd burrowed down into the snow to find. I'd watched him cocking his head this way and that as he listened for movement beneath the snow before he pounced and began tossing the hapless victim about. Perhaps it was a field mouse he'd caught. Or maybe a small pack rat. There's no shortage of either here 'bouts. We could certainly attest to that when the ceiling insulation in our basement fell down because of the weight of all the sunflower seeds that'd been secretly stashed away there. Talk about one seed too many!

Anyway, as you can probably tell, I've lots and lots of stories about living out here in the mountains, but I don't want to digress from the issue of this chapter. The balance of nature is a concept of great substance.

Life versus death.

Life-giving spring rainfall versus torrential flooding.

Sweet and fragrant breezes carrying seeds versus destructive tornadoes.

Lightning strikes causing forest fires versus new life springing from the ashes.

Every nature element carries the potential for the desired positive and the conversely dreaded negative effects.

Balance.

Our ten-acre property is not flat land. It's oddly shaped, and when we walk it we ascend ridges and descend into several valleys. Our driveway follows a ridge up to the road where massive spruces and firs grow on the downsloping side. Last summer when Sally and I were out cutting deadfall for our winter firewood, we came upon a most disheartening sight. Dozens of these magnificent trees had been felled by the powerful winds that blow up from the valley floor. These downed trees were so colossal that a person could almost make a survival cave within one of their masses of roots, which stood twelve feet high. Standing beside such a tangle was humbling.

Everywhere we looked, we saw more and more perfectly healthy spruces and firs tipped at every conceivable angle, some horizontal. They were so huge that we couldn't reach their trunks with the chain saw unless we began our cutting at the very top end of one of the trees that had actually made it all the way to the forest floor. We were sickened at the devastation. A century-old tree–dozens of century-old trees–is toppled by a sudden microburst. That seems sad. Indeed, it's very sad. Yet those very same trees that are not culled by woodcutters decompose and lend their many nutrients to the forest floor. When they don't create warmth for us in the winter as firewood, they create rich mulch, in which a multitude of new botanicals spring to life.

Balance.

Give and take. Offer and receive.

The offering of self so that others may receive sustenance to survive and thrive. It's Nature's way of gifting itself in order to maintain a fine balance to the entire flora and fauna ecosystem. In nature death is frequently an offering–a gift–that ensures the continuum of life. This is Nature's way.

The way of human life is no different. Human nature and all it encompasses present us with an endless variety of emotions, situations, attitudes, experiences, and psychological compositions that serve to balance our lives just as nature is balanced. When people ask, "Why do bad things happen to good people and good things happen to bad?" they're really saying that they don't understand how nature works. Though it would appear that certain events in life are random or unfair, we need to ask ourselves this: *From whose perspective is this specific event being viewed to make it appear good or bad?* For instance, a wealthy woman wins the Power Ball lottery. That can be good or bad, (fair or unfair) depending on the perspective of the winner or the losers. See what I mean? Or the tornado that rips through a town and wipes out entire blocks of residential homes yet leaves two standing completely untouched. Two residents will feel lucky or blessed while all the others, who've lost everything, ask, "Why me, God? Why us? Why my home?" There is no answer to these questions because they're not valid queries. God doesn't point a finger and create destruction. A tornado can't think or choose which direction it takes or which homes it skips over. God has nothing to do with it because nature is as nature does. There's no analytic thought behind whether the date for a planned picnic will turn out to be a bright, sunny day or one dark with thunderheads that threaten the fun.

Nature is as nature does. I can't say that enough because too many people make attachments to nature's ways. They turn nature and its workings into a personal issue by blaming God or shifting the responsibility for an event, relationship, or experience gone bad. We've all witnessed this behavior time and time again, yet we forget that many of these situations were brought about through personal choice. We complain about our jobs, yet we were the ones who filled out the applications. A cut of meat is tough and the butcher is blamed, yet the shopper was the one who chose that cut. Human nature is balanced by the additional presence of free-will choices. Those who choose to live in the Midwest, knowing that it's also called Tornado Alley, and those who choose to live in earthquake country cannot blame God for a geologic event or an adverse weather phenomenon that causes destruction to personal property or culminates in a loss of life.

Human nature, like the nature of nature, possesses polarity. By this I mean that human attitudes, psychological makeup, emotions, and thought processes can contain both positive and negative elements. No emotion exemplifies this concept more than love. This is because no emotion is more bipolar than love. It's the most manic-depressive emotion there is. It can cause one to soar up to the farthest star one night and plunge one into the depths of depression and despair the next. Love possesses the positive and negative elements within its essence. Therefore, love can either hurt or give a warm and cozy sense of rightness. It can make one feel empty or it can fill one with an overwhelming sense of having everything right. One can feel that the love one is giving (or receiving) is shallow, obligatory, or all that it can and should be.

One of the amazing facets of love is that the more deeply

it's felt, the greater the hurt it can cause. It's very much like the saying "The higher you are, the harder you fall." The fuller the glass, the more is spilt when it's dropped. Its ripeness can be deliciously sweet when love is in its positive stage, or it can turn terribly bitter when it's in the negative stage. And this is why love is the single human emotion that is bipolar. It has the ability to perch on either end of the psychological teeter-totter, depending on the events the relationship.

Ahh, love, what a sweet, sweet nectar it has. But love isn't the only emotion in our lives. We have disappointments and joys. We experience sadness and happiness. We're up one day and down the next. We take it as it comes and deal with it. We deal by acceptance and by recognizing the fact that life is, indeed, balanced. And it's all in how we look at it. We can look at life with knowledge and understanding or we can go around kicking the furniture and cussing at it. It's up to each one of us to discover that valuable, psychological path called Happy Medium that allows us to accept the disagreeable along with the good.

Sure, bad things happen to good people. Sure, good things happen to the bad ones too. But that just gets us back to realizing that life has a balance and, from that jumping-off point, we gain an understanding that that dynamic recognition is a powerful tool–it can be the Great Equalizer in life if you will let it be. It can bring rationality and reason into every situation you come up against.

This equalizer is wisdom, the wisdom to know about and thoroughly accept the reality of nature. Those who decry their lives with an eye to the shadows of fate will say that nothing good ever happens to them or that there's never anything to be happy about. This perspective takes us back to those who perceive a half-filled glass as being only half empty instead of both half empty and half full. These folks would rather look at a situation and see only the shadows rather than the *light* that *caused* those shadows. In essence, they can't see the light for the shadow it casts.

In reality, nature has no dark side, only a *balancing* side. This balancing aspect serves to maintain equilibrium. An example is when an earthquake happens somewhere in the world and, shortly afterward, another one will occur or a volcano will begin to let off steam in a different region. This is nature balancing the release of its internal pressure. Likewise, we humans have our bad days balanced out by our good days. Or a disappointment will suddenly be elevated to joy after the appearance of an unexpected factor.

Life is full of ups and downs. The trick to riding those rolling waves is to have the wisdom to understand that they are balanced by equal movements and avoid perceiving only the ones carrying you down into the troughs.

The coyote at play is not a sign of nature's dark side but rather a sign of the precious gift of balance that the Old Woman of the Woods lovingly shares with all of her children. We, too, can benefit from this special gift of balance if we have the wisdom to recognize it whenever we come across it.

autumn afternoon—life cycle celebration

HAVE YOU EVER WISHED YOU COULD LIVE FOR-ever within one very special moment—as if you had some magical power to still-frame it? Maybe you've experienced the exhilarating feeling of love in full blush and wanted it never to change or fade. Perhaps one momentous or wondrous phase of your life seemed so perfect in every way that you wished with all your might you could preserve it in time. Or what about enjoying a festive gathering around a crackling fire on a snowy Christmas Eve, having all your loved ones around you, hearing their laughter, and feeling the warmth of shared familial bonds? Possibly you've had this desire to freeze-frame an experience or time while you've been enjoying the ideal vacation, away from the daily grind.

This thought could even have come to mind as you walked out your door and were greeted by a particularly beautiful summer morning when sweet birdsong soothed your heart and a warm breeze caressed your cheeks, leaving behind the fragrant sign of Mother Nature's recent visitation upon your person–the pungent perfume of flowers in full bloom.

I think we've all had times such as these when we deeply desired that everything would always remain as perfect as it was right then. In these special moments we find ourselves enveloped with happiness or at least a full sensation of well-being. A contentedness, a peacefulness surrounds us. It's those times when we feel as if a magic potion mystically made everything in life "just right." When we want to leisurely absorb every facet of the moment and bathe in its warm waters forever.

This is the way I feel about autumn. Ohh, how I love to immerse myself in the forest during its awesomely sensual season when the Old Woman of the Woods shows Her most stunning attributes. Nature's beauty makes me so giddy, so dizzy and dreamy that my old mentor used to grumble that autumn filled my head with woodsmoke! She'd grump at me to get back down to earth and be more mentally focused. Phooey to that, I'd think. Autumn lasts only a short time up in this high country and, by God, I was gonna soak up every facet of it like a human sponge! So what if it made me giddy? So what if I lost mental focus and turned a bit scatterbrained during the fall? What cared I about that when my heart, mind, and soul were singing and my body was swaying and twirling about with absolute joy for just being alive? To my way of thinking, there was plenty of time to be centered, to put my intellect to the grindstone, to ponder the deeper realities of life.

During autumn–then and now–all I want to do is lose myself in the grandeur of pure joy. All I care about is giving myself over to the seduction of the senses that I so easily fall into. What harm is there in that? What harm is there in wishing it'd last . . . forever? Woodsmoke in my head? Yes, oh *yes*! Bring it *on*! Bring on all autumn's tantalizing qualities that so completely fill my head like those sweetly frosted sugarplums dancing in the heads of all those children while they dream their sweet dreams on the night before Christmas.

There's nothing like standing on the forest floor and gazing up into a golden aspen or red maple leaf that's backlighted by the brilliance of the sun. With the incredible blueness of the sky as the ceiling, it's just like looking up through stained glass. The woods in autumn is Mother Nature's sanctified cathedral, where all of creation's living sacredness worships the eternally loving Creatrix. Indeed, to me, autumn is the most festive ceremonial time, when all of nature rises to perform and celebrate its most sacred rites of the year.

Entire mountainsides join the annual celebration by donning their ritual robes of shimmering spun gold generously studded with sparkling rubies, twinkling emeralds, and gleaming garnets. Such grand attire dazzles the eye and swells the heart. It inspires the soul to soar up into a place of sacred, heightened awareness where the simple quaking of the aspen leaves is heard as a multitude of tinkling temple bells, and the wonderfully new scent in the air is the magical, intoxicating incense that fills the entire land with the knowledge that this is indeed a sacred time.

Nature's ritual participants are proudly wearing fiery reds. Blazing orange and gold flares emanate from Mother Nature's glorious aura. This time, this spectacular autumn time, is when the Old Woman of the Woods shines like the guiding lodestar that She is, as Her inner beauty turns into a glorious visual for all to see with their soul eyes and feel with their hearts.

Ohh, yes! The sunny rays of autumn afternoons mysteriously dance and twirl with purpose while they coalesce to spin the fibers of the magic carpet that gently sweeps me off my feet. It sweeps beneath my feet and floats me up through dizzying heights where simple reality merges with that of the profound–the Old Woman's soul–and there I'm invited to sup from Her personal golden cup of autumn's intoxicating elixir. And so I am transported in mind and body to the soft, ample breast of autumn's peaceful quietude to rest a spell. I willfully submit to Her nurturing care and Her lilting chants that drift in whispers from Her sweet breath as cooing lullabies coming to soothe the so very world-weary soul.

Upon awakening, I find myself refreshed and eager to be an active participant in Her wild rites of autumn. I'm ready to join in the enchanting dance around the bonfires of flaming leaf colors that leap high into the air like ignited fireworks and then rain down their twirling sparks onto the ground where I stand. My heart, overflowing with such wonder, laughs and giggles like a small child and, stretching out my arms, I try catching some of the sun-ignited embers before they die out at the touch of the cool forest floor. I'm caught up in the enchantment, and I'm well aware of both my actions and my voluntary abandonment to autumn's charms. I care not a whit if, by an unforeseen happenstance, I should be observed by some unknowing outsider who's never felt the magically seductive kiss of the Old Woman of the Woods upon her cheek. I care not if such an unaware (and unfortunate) individual witnesses my wild dancing and overhears my laughter and then considers me quite mad. Ah, more's the pity for the poor, hapless wanderer who unsuspectingly loses her way and finds herself within the autumn magic of my enchanted woods.

Ah, never is Mother Nature as luscious as She is as when She's in Her autumnal prime and so full of playful seduction.

Woodsmoke in my head? Oh, nay. Oh, no, I think that my old mentor couldn't really have meant that, for her wisdom was great and she had to have had the knowing that I see and feel with more clarity in autumn than during any other time of year. Perhaps that was the real meaning behind her continual admonitions. Perhaps my old visionary friend cleverly kept her intent hidden behind the mask of disciplinary comments until I myself truly understood the full power of Mother Nature's autumn attributes.

No. No sooty woodsmoke clouding up this one's head during the spectacular season of Mother Nature's blazing display of Her womanliness. No, no, only joy . . . pure unadulterated abandonment to and uninhibited joy taken from Her magnificent beauty and my soul's celebration of the same.

Ahh, autumn. A season of long, drawn-out, dreamy sighs and ecstatic pleasures of the soul if ever there was one.

Autumn, obviously enough, is the one aspect of life that I wish I could freeze-frame. Clearly, like many of you, I too desire to live forever in a very special time that's so dear to my heart and soul. Would that we could. Would that it could actually be such a wonderful possibility without having to obtain some secret potion of Morgan le Fay's, or without having to perform anything more complex or magical than the simple, soft utterance of the whispered words of one's secret wish. Sigh.

So now we've reached the stage in this colorful narrative where we find ourselves having to come face-to-face with the disappointing wall of cold, hard reality and . . . *deal* with it. But is it? Is reality truly a cold, hard wall to have to deal with? Isn't reality more of a continuum of life? Isn't it a grand Circle of Cycles that we all pass through as we strive to grow intellectually, emotionally, and spiritually, and progress toward physical maturity and philosophical wisdom?

There is little appreciation felt for a rainfall without the long dry spell that preceded it.

A time of inner serenity is never more deeply relished than when it comes on the heels of a time of strife and tribulation.

A clear blue sky is rarely counted as a divine blessing until it seems to appear miraculously following a week of nonstop, torrential rains. So what's all that got to do with the real-world reality of those circling cycles? Everything. Absolutely everything.

As much as many of us would dearly love to experiment with that stop-action, freeze-framing thing, and even if we succeeded, it ultimately wouldn't turn out to be the paradise place we'd thought we'd put ourselves in. Why? Because, eventually, routine becomes the mundane, and the mundane quickly slumps into monotony, and . . . boredom sets in.

You see, a great deal of what makes those autumn afternoons that I love so special is the fact that they're part of a cycle–one of the seasons–that I eagerly look forward to. If all seasons were autumn time, what would make autumn so unique? And, if all seasons were autumn, where would the joy of watching the springtime crocuses and hyacinths peek up through the warmed soil be found? Where would the coziness of sitting with a loved one before a cabin woodfire when a snow blizzard is howling beyond the frosted windowpanes go? And how would I replace summer picnics and hikes through the mountains quilted in fragrant wildflowers? What about all those summertime blessings I'd miss having? I think that if my favorite season were to replace the other seasons, I'd end up yearning to experience them again. I might not enjoy autumn as much as I do now, when it is fleeting.

Cycles.

Life is a circle of cycles, each presenting varying phases of life experiences, growth, and maturity.

The human cycle of life can seem complex. More than a few folks will experience it as a time to be fought through or lived in denial; to others life is a beautiful blossom unfolding. Life is a garden. How the garden looks or how it's maintained is up to each individual. This visual of one's garden and its care is directly related to how one perceives life. If one hates life and fights it tooth and nail, then one will have no blossoms of acceptance blooming in the garden. If one looks at life through the lenses of negativity, the garden will reflect that attitude by being full of disease and insect-ridden plants. Weeds will be prolific and choke out the flowers.

Life cycles of the human condition are always in motion. Sometimes this motion is so subtle that we don't realize it's happening–like the rotation of the planet. We never actually *feel* the earth turning, but we know that it is because of the sun's daily dawning and the awe-inspiring sunsets we witness. The cycles in one's life can pass just as quickly as the days and be felt as little as the turning of the earth.

Right from the time we take that very first birth breath until the time we make the slow exhalation of our last, we gently move through many successive cyclic phases; some are minor and fragile in their simplicity, while others are full of dynamic emotion and are always remembered as pivotal points.

Infanthood, during which our every physical and emotional need is provided for by a parent or other adult is the first cycle.

Childhood is when we become cognizant of the ego and tentatively begin realizing that we're separate individuals, when we stretch our sprouting personalities and start learning how to interact with others.

The teenage years, when the buds of independence and a more solid sense of self take form, are often fraught with turmoil from both multilevel internal conflicts and outside relationships as the teen strives to discover and express that unique identity called Self. This often dramatic teen phase is compounded by a variety of elements, such as the new squeeze of peer pressure, acquisition of a greater awareness of the world and, consequently, facing the existence of warring nations, the threat of nuclear utilization, the knowledge that terrorists are turning to germ warfare, as well as having to choose a career in which to support oneself during the next cycle of life, which is fast approaching.

Adulthood is the life cycle that offers the widest variety of choices. As adults we make choices about schooling in endless fields of higher learning, we choose where we would like to live. Adulthood offers greater opportunities to grow intellectually and philosophically; to expand and round out one's knowledge, one's personality, and its many avenues of expression; and to deepen (or lessen) one's wisdom depending on whether one recognizes and cherishes the powers of tolerance and acceptance. Adulthood is when most familial bonds are formed. It is when we choose to marry or remain single and also make the choice about becoming parents. Parenthood, if chosen, will be deeply intertwined with almost every other element during this stage of life.

Elderhood. Ahh, now we come to the autumn years, when life can be an extended phase of full-time celebration. This is the cycle wherein the proverbial piper's already been paid by putting in our many years of nine-to-five time. And, I might add, that piper was indeed well-paid. Now a great deal of one's life responsibilities become noticeably lessened. There's more quiet time to fully enjoy those little personal pleasures or hobbies and leisure activities that the familial or career obligations of the former cycle left few hours for. Elderhood is the cycle of gentleness–one of grace, especially if all the preceding cycles left one with a mellowness evolved from good measures of wisdom and acceptance.

So we see that each life cycle holds specific changes within itself. Each presents challenges to tackle, and each offers heart-welling blessings to cherish.

In infancy we enjoy the convenience of having all our needs taken care of and, one hopes, we're loved so much that we're treated like precious treasures.

In the childhood cycle we have those special days of trembling anticipation, maybe the excitement of trying to sleep on Christmas Eve, or a memorable birthday party, or that first summer camp, or perhaps going fishin' with Grandma at her lakefront cottage.

The teen years are full of pals and secrets shared. These years present gifts of self-discovery and the realization that one's whole life is ahead. The first kiss, getting the driving permit, that magical sweet sixteen birthday, the prom, the joy of expressing one's individuality in diverse and outrageous ways, and flying out of the nest to college or into an apartment of one's own.

Adulthood presents the most opportunities because it spans so many years. Breaking a personal record, regaining control over some facet of one's life that had slipped away, rediscovering love when you'd thought you'd never love again, being an activist for some cause you feel passionate about, and working to make a difference in the world are all examples of the achievements and events that can come during the adult cycle of life.

And elderhood–holding one's first grandbaby, teaching a grandchild how to handle a garden trowel, lazy afternoons spent holding hands with your loved one while rocking on the porch watching a fiery sunset that slowly settles to a warm ember glow like the love in your hearts. Or the both of you having the time to toil in the garden and then share laughter about your old, creaky bones and how neither of you is a spring chicken anymore.

Every cycle in the human life has its unique aspects, yet I believe the most difficult phase is not the teen years, as most people think, but rather the adult cycle, particularly the latter phase, frequently referred to as *midlife*. Some folks do well while others have a rough time getting through it.

We hear so much about the "midlife crisis." But you know what? I'm going to let you in on a little secret. If folks didn't focus so much of their attention on their egos at this age, there'd be no such thing as midlife crisis. But the latter portion of the adulthood cycle involves that allegedly dirty word that often brings fear and high anxiety along with it. That dreaded word is *aging*!

Mmmm, aging.

For men, the hairline begins receding and it takes more concentrated effort to keep holding that ol' stomach paunch in where it belongs. They spend more time in front of the mirror, noticing the development of jowls. The arm muscles are flexed more often and the pecs are inspected on a daily basis. All of these lead to the question men ask their reflections in their mirrors: "Do women still want me?"

So they make it their quest to discover the answer. They buy new clothing in an attempt to present a more youthful impression with current styles. The family van is often traded in for a sporty car (flaming red, of course) or for one of the biggest, most macho SUVs (black because black is *bad*). A trip to the barber may no longer be as satisfying as it once was; now the youth-seeking man frequents a "hair stylist" who will feed his starving ego with just the cooing compliments he's craving.

When this man thinks he's staved off the appearance of aging, he'll take his new aesthetic guns out to test them on any likely target who catches his eye. If he's married, this is called infidelity. If he's not, it's called playing the field, or at least trying to.

For women who possess strong egos and a distorted perception of true beauty, the recognition that gravity takes over those once firm portions of the body can be devastating. These women will resort to any magic cosmetic potion sold on the late-night infomercials or spend countless dollars on visits to the surgeon's body shop for all the nip 'n' tucks, suctions, implants, and collagen injections their egos desire. They, too, change their clothing style to either a more youthful one or a more traditionally classic one, depending on who they plan to impress with their newfound personae.

This type of woman will cringe if anyone should mention the fact that she's a grandma. Like her male counterpart, she'll tend to trade in the family sedan for a Miata (red). She won't be inclined toward the SUV, but perhaps a BMW will catch her eye. She may begin jogging or making routine trips to the local health club or spa and be sure to drink only the bottled water while she's there. Of course she'll dye her hair to conceal those unsightly gray strands.

Both genders caught within this fear of aging syndrome develop complex emotional problems because they're in denial of their natural beingness–they don't want to accept matured age. Their behavior robs them of the benefit of maturity by reducing them to immature individuals who run themselves ragged trying to alter the reality of their lives. And it really is pitiful to see these people spend so much effort and expense on their denials.

Aging and its beginning signs is a substage. It's the final bridge between adulthood and elderhood. It can be voluntarily approached and easily crossed with the lighthearted Song of Acceptance in one's heart, or it can be dreaded as though it were a swinging rope bridge over the churning waters of the river Styx.

Wisdom and acceptance have no effect upon this fear of aging as long as the individual remains focused on the ego. All the wisdom and acceptance in the world cannot preclude this fear if one loves self above all else. In fact, it could even be said that *wisdom* and *ego* cannot be used in the same sentence, because their concepts are in direct opposition to each other. They are as oil and water–never to be integrated within one mind-set.

Daily we witness evidence of humankind's vain efforts at staving off aging, and its love affair with beauty and youth. Aging is rarely perceived as a gentle life cycle filled with grace and respect. When was the last time you heard that someone's goal in life was to age, or to become an elder? How often have you heard a woman *wish* for all her hair to be silver? More likely you've heard someone wish to shave ten years or more off his or her age. So, why is this? What is this fascination with youth and fear of aging? What's making this beautiful life cycle of adulthood such a dreaded natural stage? What makes many of those in the latter stage of adulthood fight like pit bulls to hold on to their last shreds of youth?

Perhaps these individuals believe that the inevitable signs of aging make them appear less attractive, less appealing in some way. Is it that they want to be noticed in a crowded room? Do these folks equate aging with reduced respect for oneself? Do they believe they won't get as much attention as they once did when they presented a virile or desirable appearance? Doesn't that sound awfully self-absorbed? Terribly shallow? Sure, it does. In fact, it sounds downright ignorant because it's just like the cute little child who always wants to stay a child because she gets so much attention, so many presents, so much cooing over. She hears the cooing sounds and has come to love them–actually to crave them like an emotional addiction–because they feed her ever-hungry ego, which is never completely satiated.

And so it is with many latter-stage adults. They cannot find the grace of acceptance to move smoothly forward. Without being able to hold their wonderful silvery heads high, they cannot make themselves take a last look back and laugh at life. They cannot manage this simple act because they fail to recognize the beautiful dignity that's their right to claim with the coming of aging. Their rite of passage is freely offered, yet they decline their ticket.

Declined with denial or accepted with grace makes no difference–aging is unavoidable; eventually, we all board the boat to elderhood. Whether the passenger perceives that boat as a sinking dinghy or a luxury cruise liner is relative to personal perspective on the reality of life coupled with perception of self.

Priorities.

Self or reality.

Denial or acceptance.

Calm waters or rough seas.

We all have those choices when it comes to crossing the aging threshold.

Few haven't heard of the phrase "the terrible twos" when referring to the often tantrum-filled behavior of a two-year-old child. Some folks will swear that the teenage years are the worst to go through. Others will believe that life won't ever get back to normal until their last child reaches the age of eighteen, gets a job, and moves out on her own. Yet, as I've described, I believe that the latter part of adulthood is the hardest for many people because they have such a skewed idea of beauty and of the truly *attractive* qualities in people. Folks are completely blind to what a great gift and blessing fidelity to one's lifelong lover is despite all the naturally occurring changes in physical appearance. They have no recognition of true wisdom's quiet dignity, and the fact that it is gained from many years of experiencing both tragic and joyful life events.

On some subconscious level, everyone is cognizant of these sequential life cycles. When the teenager says, "I don't want to graduate because I'm having so much fun with all my school friends," it's the same as saying, "I don't want to go out into the scary world and leave the comfortable atmosphere of school and lose all my friends when they drift their own ways." The student isn't ready to give these friends up in exchange for a new circle of the working world. There are students who've made a career of college because they don't want to leave the secure circle of the school setting that they've become so comfortable in.

Each life cycle represents a new stage that's enclosed in a very real circle of an entirely new environment, a new set of social and worldly circumstances, strangers to form relationships with, situational elements to face and deal with–the *unknown,* which one must enter and come to know. These are likened to nature's annual seasons of change. Springtime symbolizes new beginnings and youth. Summer is associated with one's prime of life, when all the social, career, and philosophical blossoms have opened and time and energy are concentrated on the maintenance of one's personally designed garden. Autumn is the transition portion of adulthood's end stage of quiet wisdom and acceptance that fully prepares us for entry into the elderhood cycle. And winter designates that final life cycle that represents our long-awaited time of rest and leisure, full of warm memories and counted blessings.

There's no doubt that, out of all the splendorous seasons of nature, my excitement grows as autumn approaches here in this high mountain country. If I sometimes wish autumn would never end and hope that its prime of regal robes and spectacular glory will go on forever, I also know that the greater portion of my joy is in the anticipation of its arrival. A constant season of autumn would negate my anticipation and wild excitement over each sign of its approach. In having an autumn that continued, I'd be lessening the ultimate ecstasy I've always reaped from its peak time.

So, would I really want to freeze-frame autumn's prime? Forever? No, I definitely wouldn't want to do that, because autumn is only one of the hugely dynamic arcs within nature's life cycles, and to want to exist within only one of them denies me the wonderful blessings and joys that can be reaped from all the others. All the seasons are loaded with rich elements that offer untold opportunities to grow, learn, and mature into deeper wisdom. Freeze-framing autumn would be like voluntarily cheating myself through conscious denial.

Each of us must pass through life's natural cycles to become a better human being. Autumn afternoons are a delicious celebration of life for me, yet so is the excitement of spying the first wild crocus poking its lavender head out of a bed of melting snow. So too is dancing on the glittering diamonds of snow in the reflected blue light of the full moon. So too is a summer morn when I'm gently nudged awake by a fragrant breeze softly carrying the morning chant of a multitude of birds from the trees outside my bedroom window.

Ahh, yes, those sensuous autumn afternoons are but one morsel that satisfies my hunger. I'm always ready to sample the delectable offerings on every season's full banquet table.

the enchanted forest—the child within

IF YOU'VE EVER HAD THE OPPORTUNITY TO BE around small children you've found that their general opinion of adults greatly differs from those we hold of ourselves. When I was a dance teacher I'd take the time to get to know some of my young students while we were waiting for their mothers to pick them up after class. We'd talk about all sorts of things, everything from their favorite activities and hobbies to what they thought was right and wrong with the world and how they would change it. What impressed me the most was the children's candid outspokenness, their lack of hesitancy to express themselves, and the absence of fear that they might say something I'd laugh at or criticize them for. They seemed to have some inner sense that they could trust me with their thoughts and feelings. One little girl in particular was so honest that she hugged me right before saying, "You have a witchy nose." I smiled and told her I knew that, then pointed to my chin. "I have the chin to go with it!" She laughed hard as little girls will do and then became very serious when she added, "Don't worry, Miss Mary, I still love you."

Throughout my many years' experience with children, I've come to note that they tend to perceive most adults as stuffy, distracted, and, well . . . a bit stodgy. These young ones see grown-ups as far too physically busy and mentally preoccupied to listen to them or to play a game, much less stoop to share an experience of pure make-believe. I've also noticed that the mainstream adult imagination has been suffocated by the continual grind of dealing with the hard-core aspects of daily reality.

Too busy.

Too tired.

Too serious.

Too preoccupied.

Too stifled.

Too worried.

And having no fun, just no fun at all.

Why is this so? Why is this reality of adult life so obvious even to the littlest child? How is it that the young ones in our lives oftentimes see so much more clearly than we do? Have a greater awareness of the subconscious reasons behind our behavior? Possess a sixth sense that's attuned to our moods and quasi-hidden attitude of the day? I find this awareness interesting (and disturbing) because we, as adults, have often given little credence to children's perceptual abilities.

So, again, I repeat the question, Why is this? What is the big mystery behind adults appearing so serious and uptight all the time? I'm sure people realize how stressed they are, because it's really hard to ignore all the signs. Look at how that inner tension has manifested itself in our unpleasant actions–snapping at children, being rude to strangers, and creating road rage to name but a few. Could the mystery be that adults have completely ignored their Child Within? Could the solution to our adult stodginess and stress be as simple as recognizing that Child Within and acknowledging all the wonderfully carefree and innocent qualities that child is just itching to release in a burst of exploding joy?

It seems to me that folks are like balls of twine–the soft core hidden within a tightly bound string of ego that gets longer every day as it builds the ball larger and larger, making it heavier and heavier to lug around. Imprisoned within that ugly ball–right in its center–is that emotionally sensitive and impetuous part of themselves that's crying out to have a chance to experience life and freely express her or his natural responses to it.

Everyone has a Child Within. If you think that's just a bunch of hooey, then maybe we'd better take a closer look at the concept.

That child aspect of consciousness is the fun-loving and marvelously uninhibited facet that doesn't give a hoot about ego or how some behavior *looks* to others. It doesn't care a whit what other people may think. It's the aspect of us that is the thrill seeker. It's the part of us that is never embarrassed to show those instant reactions of pure, innocent emotion, such as freely letting the tears fall while watching a sad or heart-touching movie, or laughing at the tickle of sunshine on one's face, or expressing awe at a butterfly alighting on the back of our hand.

The Child Within wants to experience all there is in life that brings out joy and gaiety. To laugh and to play. To touch everything. To skip about when the heart is happy, and to dance and twirl with autumn's spinning leaves as they fall to ground. That child notices the subtle blessings of nature that the adult suppresses. That child's giggles get muffled by the adult's sense of ego because that adult mistakenly believes if those giggles are let out, she or he will have to endure humiliation by onlookers. Many adults keep their Child Within in check because they don't want others to see them act too emotionally or spontaneously and call them crazy.

For most adults the fear that others' negative opinions may somehow damage their image is the singular block to allowing that precocious and adorable Child Within to express itself in whatever manner it chooses. This is a fear that's completely unwarranted and has no basis if one isn't giving the ego priority in life. To place the ego above all other personal concerns is to imprison oneself in a dark, musty cell in which life can never be fully experienced. It condemns one to a life of seeing only the dark, negative side of everything. It increases the incidence of melancholia and depression. It exacerbates anxiety and stress levels. It keeps joy under wraps. It buries the wholeness of self. And only the *contrived* facade of the self is allowed to be touched by the sunlight. Most folks call that living. I call it a voluntary slow death. I call it that because that's just what it is–suicide.

The American Medical Association has not been reticent about how depression, stress, anger, and suppressed emotions can contribute to physical illnesses, how these negative emotions have been proven to participate in the breakdown of the autoimmune system and in making our physiological (and psychological) systems more susceptible to the activation of recessive disease genes that could otherwise remain forever dormant. Recognizing and releasing the wonderful feelings of joy and awareness that our Child Within possesses is one of the greatest keys to better health and overall well-being.

Damn the torpedoes when it comes to ego. That ego is killing people all over the world. It's a hidden cancer that eats like a starving shark, tearing relationships to shreds. It takes over one's true identity as easily as if one had donned a masquerade costume and found one couldn't take it off. Allowing the ego to top your priority list is the same as inviting the specter of death to sup at your table. You'll never be able to be true to self, much less truly know self, because the ego you love so much has made a stifled, mechanical monster of the sensitive humanness of your core beingness. And the monster has programmed itself to suppress emotional responses, indeed, even internal sensitivity. You become desensitized to life, its inherent, natural beauty, its many precious joys, its innate wisdom. This desensitization plugs the ears, blinds the eyes, binds the heart, and clips the wings of the soul–all cherished facets of that Child Within who is so anxious to experience life to the fullest.

Most adults who make the ego their number–one interest in life don't completely succeed. They never realize that there are times when that all–important ego slips down a notch or two, when their Child Within makes a clean break for its yearned–for freedom. What am I talking about?

I'm talking about those times when the ego–loving adult laughs and screams while riding the amusement park's monster roller coaster.

I'm talking about when the adult locks himself in the basement–away from the prying eyes of his peers–and indulges in hours of playing with his system of model trains, complete with villages, mountains, tunnels, and all the related lights, whistles, and moving parts. Or when the mom slips into her little girl's room during school hours and, feeling somewhat guilty, picks up the Barbie doll and plays with it.

I'm talking about the hoots and hollers, about the silly

painted faces and the jumping up and down that's so easily displayed at football games. That type of uninhibited behavior is absolutely allowable in such situations because, of course, it's in the guise of supporting one's team and is completely accepted by one's peers, who, by the way, are doing the exact same things. The camaraderie is the element that makes it all right.

And I'm talking about the few times when I was so overwhelmed with joy at seeing snow falling in the moonlight that I ran outdoors barefoot to twirl and dance on nature's glistening, celestial blanket of diamonds. Although no one but my understanding companion witnessed this impulsive (and greatly amusing) behavior on those nights, I did happen to mention it in one of my previous books and, consequently, some readers polluted the pureness of that joy expressed by my Child Within by twisting the act into an ugly assumption that their ignorance conjured up. They thought I was claiming to be some goddess who could walk barefoot on snow without feeling the cold–akin to walking on water. How sad that attitude is. How utterly, utterly sad. And it wasn't as though I'd said I'd danced for *hours*! It was only a minute or so, just long enough to satiate my uninhibited urge to join with nature. It was only long enough to "touch" nature's magical beingness and feel blessed by its splendorous gift of beauty. Then, then I was right back inside the cozy cabin to warm my feet by the crackling fire.

These examples of how people let their "ego shields" down to allow their Child Within out of its locked room are but samplings of what I'm talking about. I know you've all experienced these times; they may even have come as a surprise. You may have suddenly squealed like a small child over something and then caught yourself and felt embarrassed. But why the embarrassment over joy? Isn't the feeling of joy as natural as spring rain?

If we all possess a Child Within, what's the purpose of hiding that beautifully unrepressed and candid facet of ourselves? Aren't people fragmenting themselves when this is done? Aren't they only presenting an incomplete beingness to the public when they deny such a viable and vital facet of their wholeness? And how is it that folks can say they know themselves well or claim they really know another when they and all those others never allow their whole beingness the freedom to express itself?

Ohh, sweet Sophia, it seems almost a crime to see the things people do to themselves for the sake of their almighty self-image. It is denial of self to smother natural reactions and responses. It's self-abuse. Indeed, it's downright masochistic behavior to hold to the rigid, false dogma that the spontaneity of their blissful, childlike expressions need be banished from their lives like some imagined demon from the smoking depths of ego's concept of hell–for the sad sake of that ego's contrived idea of decorum.

Children know. Even if you don't, the child knows. Children are acutely perceptive of the adults around them. Go ask the little children, whose eyes see clearly, whose ears hear true, and who will not fear to speak of that trueness they see, hear, and feel. Their answer regarding adults is "Stodgy." Their reply is "Upright." They respond, "No fun . . . no fun at all." And so, what are we going to do about it? We're going to explore ways in which the Child within can contribute to the feelings of happiness in one's life and to an overall sense of physical and psychological well-being.

Through a multitude of diverse experiments, researchers have validated the theory that an individual's *attitude* can be directly related to the quality of her or his *physical* being. As Above (the mind), so Below (the physical). We've probably all heard of this axiom but perhaps not spent all that much time thinking about what it really means. We know, but do we *really* know? And if we believe we really know, how much solid credence do we give it? Enough to apply it to our daily lives? Enough to integrate it fully into our philosophy of living? Or does it end up being one of those many bits of trivia we so casually shove into the back of our minds' file cabinet and never give another thought?

As Above, so Below. If we deny ourselves the outward expression of those wonderful, spontaneous feelings that spark many times during our week, how are we ever to have any happiness in our lives?

Happiness. Laughter. Happiness and laughter. Childlike joy.

It's not necessarily an apple a day that keeps the doctor away, but a good dose of daily laughter very well could. Having a sense of humor can put a whole different spin on things. What? You say you don't have a sense of humor? I don't buy that for one minute. I know I've heard people say, "Oh, So-and-So has no sense of humor," but get a clue here . . . all people do. If they dig way, way down and reach far back into their psyches, they'll find one. All they have to do is cultivate that sense of humor, nourish it through routine care and utilization, so that it grows toward the light of day.

Children can spontaneously laugh at almost anything that happens to tickle their fancy. Why shouldn't adults have a similar response to their world? Releasing the Child Within is not the same as relinquishing one's level of maturity. This is not a cause and effect type of phenomenon. Nurture your sense of humor. Laugh more often. When you find yourself perceiving that glass as half empty, see the rest of it as being half full of amusement. There is a lighter side to almost every situation; if you'll only turn your face toward it and use that light in a productive manner, it will benefit you greatly.

Good grief, life's way too short to be stodgy and humorless, especially when you don't have to be. Lighten up. Go shove that ugly ego into a trash can and smell the wildflowers along the wayside or in the park. Go into a floral shop to smell all the flowers. There's a whole world of joys just waiting for you to see, hear, touch, and experience with all your senses. That Child Within knows this. Why don't you? That Child Within wants to run here and there, looking at this and examining that. That Child Within wants to race pell-mell through a field of flowers, skip pebbles over pond waters, spend hours building a sand castle, burst out laughing when the urge wells from within, get up and dance around, roll in a freshly raked pile of autumn leaves, or sit in the grass to inspect the interesting dragonfly that just landed there.

We as adults have this twisted theory that maturity negates having natural, spontaneous reactions to what life offers up for our sensual pleasure. But it's that very belief that prevents us from living life to the fullest, from seeing what's there to see, from feeling the joys of a child. Unless we acknowledge our Child Within and allow ourselves the freedom to express that child's many joys, we'll never be touched by the enchantment that has the dynamic power to change our lives . . . forever after.

Enchantment.

What did reading that word bring to mind? I hope it didn't bring visuals of some scene from a sci-fi fantasy world, or make you think of King Arthur's Merlin, or maybe cowl-robed Druids gathered in a circle of monolithic standing stones. If it did make you think of any of these types of things, you'd be looking at a very limited picture.

Enchantment can be found in everyday life . . . everywhere one looks. The reason few see it is that they've lost that innocent and unadulterated wonderment of their Child Within. People notice a striking sunset while driving home from work, but few pull off the road, get out of their vehicles, and take the time to marvel at the colors. Few take the time to immerse themselves in that beauty, to join their beingness with it and feel truly blessed for having been gifted with such an awe-inspiring sight. That sunset was the kind of enchantment that would've compelled me to pull off onto the shoulder and just sit back and sigh while my eyes and soul soaked in the splendor that is such a huge part of our daily lives.

Likewise, the forages into the woodland surrounding my cabin are excursions into nature's enchanted world that can elicit a squeal of surprise immediately followed by an overflowing appreciation for the simple yet most treasured blessings that I have received. Spying a lone mariposa lily growing strong among the undergrowth can send my heart soaring. Sitting beneath a lodgepole pine and being touched by the golden sunrays spearing down through it has made me feel like I'd just been touched by a divine light. I have felt that the light has washed away all remnants of negativity that were soiling the purity of my beingness. Sometimes those rays that glitter with floating, drifting seed fluff give me the mesmerizing sense that I've been transported into a mystical world evocative of heaven. And my heart becomes full.

When I go out into the forest to gather puffballs or kindling, I go with carefully placed footsteps so as not to injure some delicate plant or crush some little critter's hidden home, for the wood is full of life secreted away in hidey-holes, burrows, tunnels, and hollow logs. Spotting a nearly invisible owl peering down at me can make my heart thud against my rib cage and send waves of joy through me before I whisper greetings to it and spend a few moments making a silent, personal communication. Enchantment. Ohh, yes, that's enchantment.

The sweet sound of a creek making its meandering way between banks blanketed with a thick carpet of soft, green moss is simply music to my ears. It soothes away the cares and any current pressures of my daily life that may have been pressing on my mind. That rippling sound has the ability to make those life elements seem not worth the stressful moments they may have caused. More effective than any relaxation tapes devised by man, nature has the capability to bring true tranquillity and the sweetest serenity into one's life. That's enchantment in its purest form, for nature can magically ground the restless mind and realign the thoughts running though it with the ordered perspective of reality.

Descending into our valley with a woven basket over my arm, I venture out with the intent of gathering a few of the wildflowers that cover the slope with stained-glass brilliance. As I scan the multitude of offerings, my thoughts are focused on which assortments I'll bundle to hang from the cabin's rafters to dry for gifts. Yet when I've entered the center of the fragrant quilt, something magical overcomes me and I forget all about why I came. The sunlight on the velvet petals like drops of shimmering dew transforms my world into one of captivating enchantment, and I begin to hum and sway in time with the blossoms, moving to and fro in the light alpine breeze. The swaying automatically shifts to the motion of a slow turn. The turn accelerates into a twirl, and I hear myself begin to giggle. I prance about the field of flowers, their fragrance becoming an inebriating incense that I breathe in deeper and deeper. A song erupts from the laughter, and I'm transported into a land of enchantment where all my senses are so overloaded that I fall into a euphoric state and wish my mate were there to make love with.

This is the Child Within's completely uninhibited response

to the natural world and the resulting soul's responsive receipt of the greatest and fullest sensations of happiness that accompany it.

Seeing the sun backlighting a delicate flower petal and noticing the tiny veins running through that simple petal can be like feeling the effects of a hallucinogen. Seeing with the clearly perceptive eyes of the Child Within places one on an emotional, sensual high like no other. It alters one's perception of the world and everything in it. It bestows clarity.

My Child Within yips and jumps up and down to finally see a baby sprout pop up out of a tray of seedlings that I planted and kept in the brightly lit kitchen window. When I planted a tray of red poppy seeds I checked them several times a day. Seeing the tiny green sprouts reaching their heads up to the sunrays coming through the window sent my heart through the roof. That's the inherent power of one's Child Within. It can transform melancholia into elation . . . in an instant. That child can change people's lives, it can change the world, but only if people will shed their tough skin of ego. That child can make folks see that proverbial glass as being half full instead of half empty. That child can cause people to see more of the golden sunlight instead of the many dark shadows it casts. That child is the bringer of renewed hope and deeper faith. That child within everyone is the most dynamic facet of personality, yet people sacrifice it for the sake of ego and the attending fears of being embarrassed or humiliated by its precocious and innocent, natural expression of pure emotion.

Suppressing the Child Within is terribly sad because it's a voluntary choice. What a shame. What a dirty shame, because people who suppress their childlike behavior are missing out on so much sensuality, the kind that can be the most potent psychological medicine available on the planet.

Now, in my imagination, I hear some people smirking and

grumbling something like "Oh well, sure, *she* can say all that about how enchanting nature is and how great it is to give free rein to her Child Within, she lives up in the *mountains*!" Well, you know what? That's got nothing to do with it. Comments like those are nothing more than a defense mechanism–lame excuses. Whether you live in a high-rise apartment, next to a freeway, or in the country, you'll still hear birdsong. So . . . when was the last time you really chose to stop and take the time to listen to that song when you heard it? It doesn't matter if you live in the middle of a bustling metropolis; there are still parks that you can go sit in or walk through. When's the last time you looked at a ray of sunlight through a houseplant's leaves and marveled at what you saw? When's the last time you passed a quiet playground and gave in to the urge to sit on the swing and see how high you could make it go or just use it as a gentle glider and take some measure of childlike joy from the soothing motion? When's the last time you danced in a gentle summer rainfall? Purposely raised your face to catch snowflakes on your eyelashes? Or took note of all the wildflowers growing along the bank of the highway you take to work each day? How often have you stopped to really see those flowers planted along the city sidewalks, taken the time to check out their fragrance? Or admired the special way a ray of sunlight slanted through your office window?

Such simple things. Such simple things in life can change one's entire perspective from the debilitating drudgery of physical stress and negative thinking to uplifting joy and a bright attitude. People have the choice to feel free enough to truly be themselves and express that beautiful whole self–that complete self–which includes the playful and ecstatically happy Child Within.

For the childlike heart, enchantment can be found absolutely everywhere. If only all people realized that they could see the magnificent beauty and give in to the unrepressed expression of their natural feelings and responses instilled by the mesmerizing sensuality of their world. If only they opened their eyes, ears, and hearts to all that exists for their souls to sip and quench their spirits' thirst. If only they'd allow themselves to experience the enchantment in all life that their Child Within is so desperately wanting to share. If only . . .

the humming—curiosities and the quest for truth

THERE HAVE BEEN NIGHTS WHEN I'VE BEEN OUT IN the deep woods bright with silvered moonlight. While sitting beneath the towering pines that swayed and shushed secrets to the night, I've sensed a subtle and extraordinary undercurrent of sound that's difficult to describe.

Many of you have probably been beneath a high-power line and heard the buzzing it makes. Well, this oddity I sense is a bit like that. But what I hear is more of a constant, rhythmic vibration coming from the ground and pulsing up through me. Since I haven't ever read of such a thing in any nature or scientific reference material, I've come to call this phenomenon the Humming. I call it that because it just hums in a steady, low-pitched tone. And I can hear (feel) it at all times, not only after sunset. I've felt it while down on my hands and knees digging in the flower garden. I've sensed the Humming gently coursing up through the soles of my feet when I'm out collecting botanicals in the forest and also when I've been gathering basketfuls of wildflowers in our grassy valley. Yet these wild places are not the only sources of the Humming. I've also felt it while walking along a Cripple Creek sidewalk or crossing a Colorado Springs parking lot. In these two places the Humming was less noticeable, yet still there. When my bare feet touch the sweet soil or when I'm out walking in the forest in soft-soled footwear are the times the sensation is strongest.

The Humming.

Many years ago, when I first perceived this physical sensation, I mistakenly equated it with Grandmother Earth's heartbeat. When I listened more closely, there was no doubt that the curiosity indeed possessed a special kind of rhythm, but it emitted no truly metered beat. It wasn't like a heart's regular lub-dub, lub-dub, it was more constant. It sounds like the hum of an aquarium motor, or maybe a computer when it's just idling. The Humming. It is a continual vibration emitted from far within the earth itself. Subtle yet strong. This sound became so noticeable that eventually I felt fully integrated with it. It became a permanent layer of my perception. I felt as though I could reach out and touch it, incorporating the awareness of it into my physical being. It was as natural as sunlight touching my skin and then activating the melanin of those skin cells into a response. Some as yet unknown and unidentified core element of nature had affected me so completely that it became a living part of me.

I sense the Humming grow in strength just before a summer rainstorm. It's also stronger during a full moon. I feel its great power when I'm out in the woods meditating and, when I'm just out in the forest gathering kindling and such, it gives me the impression that the earth is just resting, like the soft and gentle breaths of a sleeping babe. Though it be peacefully resting, it's still there. Power at rest. It's always there. It's always there . . . humming. Is this very perceptible facet of reality actually the vibrational frequency that our planet gives off? Is it related in some manner to the earth's magnetic fields? Is it associated with some type of living essence or force that's created from the combined, coalesced mineral elements within the ground we walk upon? What is the source of this sound, this energy?

I DON'T GO FOR NIGHT WOODLAND WALKS AS MUCH AS I USED TO, but when I did go night walking on a routine basis, I could always count on being accompanied out there in the deep forest world. Woods are never really completely silent, you know.

Underbrush rustles.

Tree branches tremble with the weight of a hidden critter.

Aspen leaves quiver.

Shining eyes peer down, and glistening orbs peek up at you.

Some creatures you know are there, others remain in hiding. So even though you may be the only *human* moving about out there in the moonlit forest, you're certainly not the only living *being* out there. Although you may not notice, the woods are loaded with all manner of nocturnal furry and feathered beings. And . . . other kinds, too.

During several of my night walks I've been accompanied by specks of light that appear to dance about in the air. They don't seem to be confined to a specific height off the ground—they flit above my head while gracefully weaving themselves between branches, or they are down low moving about in the underbrush, or they float at eye level and seem to hover there.

These little lights are as difficult to describe as the Humming is. They look like sparkles when seen from a distance, yet when they move closer to me they appear more like a shining aura surrounding a core essence that moves. Up close they are a mobile form activated into precise movements by intent . . . purpose. The lighted aura surrounding these tiny, living forms is too bright to look at directly. What I'm trying to convey is that the light itself prevents a clear view of the moving form at its core.

Dancing lights.

Living sparkles of glowing orbs.

What's even more interesting about these lights is that they are not unique to the darkness, that is, bound by the night. They can be seen during the daylight hours, too. It's just that, in the sunlight, they're not nearly as noticeable. At night they stand out against the best contrasting backdrop.

No sound whatsoever comes from these twinkling lights. At least, I've never heard sounds of any kind. No humming. No fluttering. No whizzing whisper of air as they sometimes speedily move about, avoiding collision with branches and such as they spin around trees and through the dense underbrush.

I've not noticed any set number of these lights when they appear. At times there may be as many as three or four dozen, and at other times there may be only one or two. The movements of the individual lights within the cluster don't seem to be tightly related to one another; there will be a group of three here, a larger grouping there, and others flitting about quite on their own. One such group of lights came approximately four feet from me. That was the closest one came except for the time a lone light zoomed up to my nose and hovered there for a few seconds before zinging off again. These lights remind me of hummingbirds that zip here and there and hover at will. Yet, as

I stated, these lights make no sound that I've ever heard. My never having heard any sound coming from these peculiar nature curiosities in no way proves that they can't make some type of sound. This is like the old question: If a tree falls in the forest and there's no one around to hear it, did the tree make a sound? Well . . . hello, of course it did. So for me to say that these unusual lights *don't* make sounds would be extremely presumptuous.

So. Where does this leave us in relation to this phenomenon of nature? Are these lights one of the Old Woman of the Woods's little secrets? Are humans permitted to perceive them in an attempt to humble our perception of what we know or *think* we know of our world's reality? One thing I do know is that these little lights are no drifting particles of swamp gas illumined by moonlight. Why, that theory would be simply preposterous.

Are they fireflies? Mmmm, then they must be fireflies that are yet undiscovered, because they don't blink on and off, and their aura of light is far brighter than that of any little lighted bug I've ever laid eyes on.

Since our cabin is in a gold-mining region, could the lights be motes of mica or minute pyrite chips that've been carried through the air in the breeze and shine when sunrays or moonglow touches them in just the right fashion? Well, I've seen mineral particles floating in the air, and these are not even close to those. These are not only not close in appearance but also not close in behavior. Besides, this shallow theory leaves out the fact that, within the core of the lights, there's some type of independent movement. Chips of mica and pyrite may twirl, spin, and gyrate at the whim of a breeze, but they surely don't have independent animation.

I'm a reasonable person. I never jump to conclusions when confronted by a sighting of something I haven't witnessed before or for which I have no mental reference. I'm a logical individual who, upon facing a new and rare experience, first tries to sift mentally through all the knowns of reality that might explain it. As I see it, there are no unexplained facets of nature or physics–only those yet undiscovered ones that patiently await the arrival of our knowledge–or our imagination–to identify them.

Impetuous judgments or presumptive conclusions made in an effort to solve the mysteries in life indicate impatience and ignorance. They're the work of those whose egos cannot tolerate a single happening that defies explanation or solution; they're the work of those who cannot permit others to think they lack knowledge of a thing. Just the way some folks believe that a rare planetary alignment signifies the end of the world or some other type of Armageddon-like event, others have a knee-jerk tendency to make an immediate explanation of our reality's oddities with any out-of-the-blue reason they can reach up and pull off the top of their heads. And this, they claim, is an expert opinion. Ahh, those ever-popular self-proclaimed mystics and psychics. They seem to have an answer for everything. I would gently caution those questing for certain answers to life. I would remind these seekers-of-answers to remember that nobody has all the answers that are being so frantically sought.

Anyway, what are those lights that dance so gracefully and glow so brightly in the depths of the mountain woods? What are those small but dynamic lights which, it would appear, no known scientific theory has identified? Or perhaps just hasn't publicly acknowledged? I have my own idea, but am not prepared to go so far as to write it down in black and white because I've no concrete proof of its validity . . . yet. Although I've been assured that one day I will have that validation, for now I'll keep my thoughts to myself on this one–just as I will on all the other experienced oddities of nature this chapter explores.

ON THE MORNING OF ONE PARTICULARLY BRIGHT DECEMBER DAY that also happened to be my birthday, I was awakened way too early by the squawking of one very loud crow that sounded as though it was directly below my bedroom window. I was more than annoyed by this bird's unneighborly behavior. The first thought that came drifting out of my foggy, sleep-ridden mind was that the bird was protecting its breakfast; perhaps it was warding off would-be usurpers of a tasty chipmunk or some other small critter that'd died during the bitter night.

Tightly covering my head with the quilt and frowning beneath the covers, I tried to recapture the sleep state I'd been yanked out of. It remained elusive as the crow continued cawing and then started in on its guttural chortling. Frustrated, I threw off the comforter and stomped across the room to the small dormer window that looks out onto the valley below. When I yanked up the blind my mouth fell open. The hair on the back of my neck stood on end and my heart lunged in surprise. The winter-bare aspens were black with crows! Saying that there were a hundred of them would not be exaggerating. What made the event even more unusual was that none of them was making a sound except the one that woke me.

A hundred crows silently perched in the tree branches outside my bedroom window was one of the eeriest events I'd ever been blessed with experiencing. All I could whisper was, "Oh, my *God*!" Then, as though they were of one mind, all of them–even the one who'd noisily wished me a happy birthday–flew off in a unified flock down into the valley.

All day long I could not get the sight out of my mind. Sally and I have a habit of keeping track of the bird species that come to our porch feeders, and we'd recorded over forty at that time. Yet never, ever, were we able to count a crow, not a single one. Shortly after my birthday sighting of all these crows, the black birds became regular visitors to our cabin and with them came their big sisters, the ravens–more like the size of ducks. We've now been gifted with quite a collection of shining black feathers left behind in the grass and snow as presents for us.

The unexpected behavior of those one hundred crows that winter morning sparked our curiosity. Sally made inquiries about crow behavior and related the incident to several of our friends who'd lived here all their lives. None of them had ever seen more than eight or ten crows gathered together at one time. My friend then asked other people, like the old-timers who frequented the local feed store. They'd shake their heads and shift their eyes as though she were overcome with cabin fever. Nope, they'd never heard of such a thing. Crows in those kinds of numbers just don't come together like that.

Yet one of our close friends is employed at one of the Cripple Creek–Victor gold mines and, after hearing our story, told us of an unconventional tale that one of his co-workers had relayed to him. The worker had some extra work to do on the mine's property one weekend. As he was about to begin working his heart sank into his stomach to see hundreds of large black crows flocking in from every direction. They silently landed on the rims of the storage tanks. Every inch of metal encircling every inch of all the tanks was lined with black birds. Never before had he seen or heard of so many crows congregating together . . . and they were just watching him. His skin broke out in goose bumps, and he hightailed it as far away from the spooky site as possible.

Clearly, from all the information we'd gathered from the nature-wise locals who have been around these parts for generations, the host of crows and ravens that had assembled themselves in a silent watch at our cabin (and the mine) were exhibiting extremely rare, in fact, downright bizarre behavior.

So here we are once again, with a facet of nature that we perceive as being a deviation from what we've come to recognize as the "norm."

These types of incidents don't usually sit well with people. Conventionality is homey. Folks like routine and dislike the unexpected or the unexplainable. Nice and neat is how they prefer it. Ordered and predictable. But is that truly the reality of Reality?

The old sourdoughs around here scratched their heads, pursed their lips, and frowned when hearing about the crow and raven visitation to our cabin, yet they also clearly conveyed that they didn't doubt it happened. They may initially have joked about Sally and me being a couple of old women who'd suffered an addle-brained condition of cabin fever, but they'd been around . . . they'd become wise to nature's ways and knew that, more often than not, oddities are the norm when nature is involved.

A hundred crows sitting in silent vigil around a lone cabin on a cold winter's morn–what's the meaning of it? Who is to say for sure? What called those birds there? And why were they all silent save one? Ahh, enigmas. What wonderful mysteries life gives us.

ALTHOUGH I'VE MADE REFERENCE TO THIS NEXT INCIDENT A TIME or two in my series of books, I feel that this chapter wouldn't be complete without reiterating it.

When I was in my late teens, my boyfriend and I had

walked to a park near my home. This park didn't have the usual amenities of a city park. It was more of a playground, with swing sets at one end and a crude baseball diamond at the other. The entire area was surrounded by chain-link fencing that separated the playing area from the backs of residential yards.

No rippling stream.

No canopy of shade trees lining meandering walkways.

No real place for chirping birds to roost.

No profusion of botanical serenity.

But for a young couple whose love was just blossoming, the place afforded a private space to sit on soft, green grass and just, well, just be together. I sat with my boyfriend behind me, his arms encircling mine. We talked about a wide variety of subjects. Finally we watched the last of the children run to their mothers, who called them home to dinner. The sun was lowering in the late afternoon sky, and our conversation waned into a warm, serene silence that seemed to bring us closer.

We shared several moments in this tranquil manner before I turned around and wrapped my arms around him. We hugged. Then I looked over his shoulder, and I froze. For there, standing in the grass behind him, was a miniature person. A small naked woman stood there staring up at me.

Maybe a foot tall, perhaps a bit shorter, the shapely woman had long black hair and a rich, swarthy complexion. Her facial expression gave no hint of her attitude; she wore no smile, no frown. Her large, almond-shaped eyes just looked deep into mine and held them locked in some kind of unnamed communion. I remember feeling no fear or dread, only the thought that I'd been gifted with something very special to carry with me through life.

Having a strong sense that the woman's visitation was a highly private affair, I didn't point her out to my companion. Instead, I quickly got to my feet and said that we needed to get going. We left the park and never returned.

Since that day I've caught myself thinking about that tiny Polynesian-looking woman more times than I can count. Her strong features, the ebony intensity of her eyes, her diminutive size and perfect proportions, all come unbidden to the fore of my consciousness.

I believe I think about this small but powerful visitor quite often because the occurrence left an indelible impression upon my psyche. And that impression is the most subtle yet dynamic one of all . . . that of the unspoken communion we shared that long-ago afternoon. Forever after I had the Knowing. A knowing that came from a firsthand experience that undeniably verified my belief in something that few others will even give one ounce of serious credence to.

Who was she? What was she? Was she some type of nature spirit who manifested into a three-dimensional vibrational frequency at that precise moment for some special purpose? Was she an illusion? A hallucination? The problem with these last two explanations is that I wasn't on any kind of drugs. I wasn't in a depressed or melancholy frame of mind, in which my subconscious may have conjured up some visual to distract me from life's woes. I wasn't in need of a psychological escape mechanism during that time or, for that matter, at any other time in my life. Besides, escapism never works because an individual eventually has to return to reality and face whatever music she or he was trying to avoid.

Who or what was the little woman I clearly saw and locked eyes with?

Another mystery. One more enigma.

THERE WAS A TIME WHEN I LIVED ALONE IN A SMALL, STONE COTtage. It wasn't purchased as a residence but rather as a place where I could spend an undisturbed part of each day converting my thoughts, feelings, and experiences into the written word. Yet destiny had other plans for that little cabin in the woods. Destiny made it available for me to live in just when I most needed it.

As it happened, the cottage was completely surrounded by a conifer forest and, in my exploratory ventures into the woods, I discovered a natural clearing beneath a tall pine that looked like the perfect prayer circle. And this is exactly how I used it. I'd be out there around eight o'clock in the morning offering up prayers. Very late at night when the moon's position was just right to send silvery beams down on the center of the circle, I'd be out there again.

My prayer times were never routine. I never followed a prescribed set of rites. There were no rituals or ceremonies. Sometimes I burned cedar incense, other times I didn't; it just depended on my mood. Spontaneity was more the rule than the exception when I walked down to the prayer circle. Sometimes I'd verbally voice my prayers, and other times I'd get into an altered state to commune silently. There were times when I'd just unburden my soul to nature itself–here I could cry my heart out to the Old Woman of the Woods, for She was a sympathetic mother. Many times I mediated in a prone position that left me quite covered with leaves. I'd return to the cottage looking like some nature sprite that'd been frolicking a bit too enthusiastically through the forest. Or I'd dance my prayers. Dance and sing a song of life. And then there were those times when I went down to the circle merely to sit on the log there and contemplate the events in my life.

Yet the core of this tale is not the prayer circle itself but what frequently appeared beside the well-worn trail leading down to it from the cabin. A black wolf would be silently sitting in the brush beside my trail and, without moving a muscle other than his neck, he'd watch my passing.

The first time I came upon him I was somewhat startled, but more, I was surprised that I'd felt no sudden fear. In fact, the more I thought about that odd reaction, the more fascinated I became. Sometimes he'd be sitting there as I began my descent to the circle; at other times he'd be present as I was making my way back up the trail to the cottage. I got so I'd pause along the way to acknowledge his presence. Although I never voiced so much as a whispered word to him, I did send him thoughts of gratitude and deep appreciation, for I came to understand that he represented some type of guardian. His aura was heavy with such an intense power that it unnerved me somewhat, yet I knew he was my friend. I couldn't tell you how I knew that . . . I just did.

In dream symbology, a wolf is associated with evasiveness and self-interest. These ideas fit in with my life at the time. I felt as though the wolf was cautioning me to evade all possible confrontations with a certain individual in order to protect myself, to give my beingness more attention and care during a most critical and pivotal time in my life. I heeded his silent message.

After I'd lived alone in this cottage for a time, my friend Sally came to reside with me. Eventually, she too saw a wolf. Although I'd never spoken about the one beside my trail, I knew both wolves were realities when she began informing me about the one she saw. The wolf she witnessed had different markings–it was not entirely black. The one she saw appeared crouched at the top of the rustic stairs leading down an embankment into another part of the cabin's woods. Sally clearly perceived this other wolf as a nonthreatening force that came to convey an unquestionable message of warning–to be watchful and careful, to keep our awareness sharply honed.

I never saw the wolf she did. And she never saw it again after that one time when she was receptive to its warning message. I suppose that, once its communication was received, it didn't need to present itself again.

The wolf I came to perceive as my guardian when I was out in the woods at night had physical substance, yet that substance was not quite the same solid mass that I was used to seeing animals have. It possessed a three-dimensional form but also appeared to have added dimensional aspects. Its eyes were wolf eyes, yet they seemed to have the great depths of the universe within them.

What kind of wolf was he? What wild wolf sits trailside and watches a human pass within three feet of it without moving anything but its head?

What sort of wolf would know the time of my passing and already be in place waiting when I arrived upon the path?

What sort of wolf has footfalls that make no sound as it moves over the heavy underbrush of a mountain forest?

Could those wolves have been some types of spirit guardians?

If you're expecting me to provide the answers for these questions, then what you're expecting to hear is pure speculation. I don't know the explanations for these curious events and manifestations any more than anyone else does. All I know is what my eyes have seen, my ears have heard, my heart has felt, and what my soul has received.

A FEW YEARS AGO WHEN I VERY MUCH NEEDED TO GET AWAY FOR a few days, Sally and I drove down to a place in South Fork, Colorado, that rented out small cabins. South Fork is in the San

Luis Valley region of the state and has been immortalized in several books that explore the area's high incidence of cattle mutilations, the presence of secret military installations, and the sightings of low-flying aircraft and unidentified flying objects.

These were not the reasons we took our little getaway in that area. We went there because friends of ours were the proprietors of the cluster of cabins and they'd invited us to come and stay whenever we felt the need to get away from it all. They were protective of my need for privacy and had assured me that no one but they would know I was there. This, of course, was an important consideration if I was to receive any measure of peace and much-needed rest. So we took them up on their kindness. During our two-day stay the local paper came out with a headline about some newfound cattle mutilations. We bought a copy to save (still have it somewhere around the cabin).

When it came time to leave town, we decided to take the long, scenic way home. We thought it'd be fun to travel through some of the high country we'd not seen before. This route would take us up past Creede, through Lake City, alongside the Blue Mesa Reservoir to Gunnison, up over Monarch Pass, and then reconnect us with the road that would take us north to Buena Vista and eastward home.

We got up early on a Sunday morning and pulled out of South Fork. We hadn't gone two miles when Sally slammed on the brakes. "Did *you* see *that*!" she exclaimed.

"See what?" I asked,

Her little Toyota Corolla was the only vehicle on the road that lazy Sunday morning, and she immediately shoved it into reverse, gunned the engine, then jerked to a stop when she aligned the vehicle with something lying on the shoulder of the road.

She got out. "Stay here," she advised. "I want to look at something."

I watched her cross the tarmac and bend down to examine a large animal carcass. After a time she motioned me over.

When I approached the deer, Sally whispered, "No visible injuries, no gunshot wound, no sign of it being hit by a passing vehicle." As our eyes met, she added, "And no flies, not a single fly on this carcass."

"Or scavenger birds anywhere to be seen," I finished.

She motioned me over to the back end of the animal. "Come an' look at this."

I stood beside Sally as she pointed down to the anal area of the deer. What I *didn't* see gave me more goose bumps than what I *did* see. I saw a perfectly round, open cavity. I didn't see any kind of crude cut marks. I didn't see any blood–fresh or old–*anywhere.* I didn't see any rectum tissue. I didn't see any flies inside. I did see a perfectly formed circular opening to a perfectly clean and empty cavity. Not only was the sight eerie but the absence of the insects and carrion birds that immediately descend on these alleged roadkills was downright spooky. There wasn't a single ant within fifty feet of the carcass.

I cursed out loud for not having brought a camera. I'd thought of it before we'd left home but purposely left it behind because this was supposed to be a completely relaxing getaway and I didn't want to be bothered with having to stop and take scenic photographs. "This is important," I said. We've got to get this on film." Sally reminded me that we didn't bring any of our cameras.

Frustrated and beginning to feel a sense of heightened anxiety, I glanced back toward town. Though the road was oddly deserted, I forced myself to remain in denial of the eeriness that began creeping up my spine. "You think a convenience store would be open and have one of those disposables?"

My companion didn't take long to mull the idea over. "You know? I have a bad feeling about this." She scanned the unpopulated, still countryside. "I have a real bad feeling about this whole thing," she repeated, looking down again at the deer and its surgically removed rectum. "We need to get outta here. Let's just go."

Hearing her verbalize what I was sensing made the hair on the back of my neck send up a signal of verification. Suddenly the idea of the photo was history.

There was no deliberation about what we'd do. In an instant we were out of there and on our way again.

As Sally drove, we decided to call our friends back in South Fork just as soon as we got to a phone. Unfortunately, we didn't come upon this idea until we reached Gunnison. Sally phoned them and suggested they go look at the mutilated *deer* we'd come across just outside their town. They said that they'd go right away.

When we arrived home several hours later, we contacted our friends again to get their take on the animal. But they couldn't give us their take on anything because there was nothing to see–the carcass had *disappeared.* Now why weren't we surprised to hear that? Someone had been very busy removing the evidence and another someone was berating herself right and left–kicking at the furniture for not having brought her camera along. Proof! Dammit! We could've had *proof*!

Yet, within a few days of our return home, both Sally and I became very ill, with a form of illness that saps away every last ounce of energy from your body. We were sick for a good three weeks. Sally's health returned more quickly than mine and she was able to cook me three wonderful meals a day that I couldn't eat or, if I did, I couldn't keep down. I ended up with double pneumonia, had extremely low blood pressure, and was bleeding from the ears. Sally carted me off to a clinic where one physician frowned after looking me over and then called another doctor to come have a look. They both scratched their heads.

"Your blood pressure's very low," one said.

I felt like saying, "Tell me something I don't know."

Thinking that perhaps I had what's called swimmer's ear, one doctor asked, "Do you do a lot of swimming?"

I told him I don't even like to get my face beneath the shower spray because I nearly drowned in a public pool when I was young. So they both took another gander at the mess in my ears. I knew what they were looking at. Although I couldn't see deep inside them myself, Sally had taken a good look with a penlight and described the small boil-like outbreaks that filled both ears. I was glad I couldn't see it.

Other than the confirmation of my double pneumonia, we received no solid diagnosis. Leaning on Sally for support, I shuffled out of the clinic with handfuls of samples of some brand-new wonder antibiotic.

I got better. It took a couple of weeks but, little by little, I got better.

As I was doing that getting well thing, Sally and I spent a great deal of time speculating on the deer experience. We concluded that the intense dread she'd been overcome with when I wanted to go find a disposable camera was generated from an inner knowing that by remaining around the carcass we were placing ourselves in a situation that could cause us physical harm. The longer we remained in close proximity to the deer, the greater the chance of illness. We came to this theory by re-examining all we'd observed.

The element that stood out as being most telling was the fact that the insects and scavenger birds knew more than we did. Their warning systems were more sharply honed than ours were. There was a critical reason why no crawling insects, flies, or birds were feeding off that fresh carcass. It was because that carcass was very different from all other roadkills. That dead deer had the same markers as the mutilated cattle linked to UFO sightings. What unseen aura could that deer have been emitting? Could it have been radioactive? The final category of questions about the carcass is related to its sudden disappearance. Why had it vanished from the area in just a few hours when, most times out in these mountainous regions, roadkills will be left to the scavengers? Who secreted it away? Where did the cleanly cut, eviscerated, and bloodless carcass end up?

I once had a lengthy conversation with a former county undersheriff who was called to the scene of a cattle mutilation. Since these mutilations are purportedly linked to UFO sightings, he told me that, after being a member of the initial investigating team, he went home and spent hours in long, hard thought. He discovered that he had a slew of unanswered questions rolling around in his head. He wanted those answers. He needed those answers.

The following day he did some checking and discovered that the carcass in question had been transported to a medical research lab outside Denver, so he journeyed there to examine the remains. When he arrived he was told that the carcass had been transported elsewhere and all pertinent information regarding the case was now out of his jurisdiction.

The undersheriff confided to me that he couldn't fully believe in the existence of UFOs until he saw one with his own eyes, yet he was denied access to the one carcass that could've answered some of his questions and, consequently, perhaps brought him closer to jumping down off that UFO fence he didn't particularly like sitting on.

Curiosities.

Oddities.

Questions. So many, many questions that remain unanswered.

Were Sally's and my strange illnesses brought on by our exposure to the deer carcass? I'd made an impulsive move to touch the carcass before Sally shouted at me not to. Instead of touching the dead animal, Sally had prodded it with a sturdy tree branch to search for any naturally inflicted wounds. Of course, as I mentioned, we found none except for the cleanly cauterized rectum incision and the equally clean removal of one eye orb.

Several research books have been written about the odd happenings and UFO sightings in the San Luis Valley of Colorado. The tiny village of South Fork is the home of many eyewitnesses whose experiences are recounted in those volumes. Questions abound and, although we have some of our own, we leave the quest for those answers to others. We prefer to leave this one alone. Still, whenever I think back on this experience, I never fail to berate myself for not having brought a camera.

SALLY AND I IMMEDIATELY DROVE OUT TO OUR CURRENT LITTLE cabin right after we had signed the closing papers. It'd been a perfect late summer day. The sunny afternoon was waning toward dusk as the sun ambled along its westward trail of deep blue sky, and we slowly walked through the empty, unfinished rooms making exciting plans for how we were going to finish them off.

Reaching the back screen door, Sally exclaimed, "You're not going to believe this! Hurry! Come look!"

I joined her at the door, and we both stepped out onto the weathered planks of the small entry porch. There, not forty feet away, were two pair of great horned owls looking down at us.

The joy that filled my heart was so profuse that I was sure it would burst right through my chest. We both softly talked to the birds while inching our way closer to them. All four owls flew into a tree further up the gravel drive.

I made my way in gentle pursuit. They, in turn, flew to perch atop the aspen branch arch that someone had built over the driveway. Then, quite suddenly, one of the owls made a swooping dive over my head, and I again verbally greeted it. The two pair returned to the trees where we first spotted them and stayed for a half hour, watching us cooing to them as we attempted to send them some sense of gentle welcome. Sally and I were so thrilled over this experience.

A week later, at about the same time of day, a friend of ours was over. She was standing on our side deck while Sally and I were on the slope beside it trying to figure out how to add the upright posts for the deck railing that had never been completed. Suddenly the two pair of owls reappeared. Our friend was awed. After that visit the owls never came again. At least if they did, they didn't show themselves.

Now what's so unique about this experience is that I feel a special kinship with owls. I've had interactions with them throughout my life, interactions that are far beyond coincidence or chance. Yet having those two pair of great horned owls appear just when Sally and I were at the cabin that first day and then having the one swoop over my head was like receiving a very special gift of welcome from a very special entity.

What brought those owls to the cabin on the very day it became our new home?

Why did they hang around with us as they did when owls are, by nature, so reclusive and nocturnal?

Why were the two pair together?

Once again we're faced with questions that are curious and confounding. Curious or not, confounding or not, I'm not about to tarnish the shine on the joy the experience blessed me with by trying to pick it to pieces to figure out all the hows and whys.

AFTER WE WERE IN OUR CABIN FOR A COUPLE OF YEARS, SALLY and I were sitting in the living room having one of our casual and highly eclectic conversations. It was nighttime, and the only illuminations that graced the cozy room were candlelight and the flickering flames of the woodstove fire. Sally, sitting on the love seat at the library end of the room, had a direct view of the front picture window. In the middle of our conversation, an odd expression came over her face. Then her eyes widened to the size of dinner plates.

The next word she managed to voice came in a stutter: "M-m-mary," she muttered, slowly rising and tiptoeing across the carpet while never taking her eyes from the window. "Mary," she whispered, "what the *hell* is *out* there?"

Having no clue what Sally was talking about (or seeing), I leaned forward and peeked out at the moonlit valley. What I saw brought icy fingertips that traced a chilling line up my spine. I quickly rose from the wingback chair and joined my companion at the window. Kneeling on the cedar chest that we used as a window seat, we peered out into the night that was now alight with . . . three floating orbs of light.

These were not just any orbs of light.

These were not those little, glowing dancing lights that seem to follow me through the night forest. Oh no, these were nothing like those miniature luminaries, nothing at all like those gay little sparkles. These were substantial objects moving freely about in the air. They were large balls of shining luminescence containing no separately defined animated core that could be discerned as with the much smaller dancing lights.

The two were as different as night and day.

One sphere was larger than the other two. The larger one looked to be about the size of one of those big plastic blow-up beach balls, and the others were more the size of hubcaps. Although they were approximately fifty feet from the front porch, it was difficult to judge their exact size. Our two pair of eyes watched in amazement as the smaller orbs seemed to circle and dance around the larger one.

The lights floated about and glided in patterns that seemed to be choreographed by some invisible dance mistress. As the large sphere floated in place with the graceful movements of a fairy princess, the other two moved around it like they were her attentive ladies in waiting. Oh, I know. You're thinking that was an outlandish analogy, but after all, I have a writer's imagination and that was precisely what the orbs' movements resembled.

"What are they?" Sally asked, without daring to take her eyes off the lights. "My God, they're right *there*! They're right there in *front* of us!"

I told her that the larger orb looked like a replica of the ball of light I almost touched as it sped over me the night the military helicopter chased it over the front porch of my other house. Recalling that incident, I shook my head and couldn't help but comment, "God, that helicopter was so low I was sure it was going to clip the roof! And another thing," I added, "why'd that sphere of light zoom right for my house, then make a hard right turn over me just as I'd raced out the door to see what all the noise was about?"

My friend shushed me. "That's all in the past. What about *these* spheres?"

"Well?" I began.

And before I could express my best guess, all three lights blinked off like someone had blown out a trio of candle flames.

Nothing was left out there but the silvery moonlight shining down on an empty valley. Well, maybe it wasn't actually empty at all, maybe there were things out there without their headlights on anymore.

Okay. So now we're back to the old routine. The questioning of what these orbs of light were.

They weren't a low-hanging aurora borealis curtain.

They weren't glowing wafts of rising swamp gas. Swamp? Here? There's no swamp within miles of our mountain cabin. I don't even think Colorado has swamps.

They weren't three lighted weather balloons. Gosh, the way the orbs moved around one another, those balloons would've ended up being one tangled mess!

They weren't jumbo fireflies.

Nor were they flying glowworms.

So? What were they?

So? Who cares? And that's the whole point of this entire chapter of "curiosities and the quest for truth."

When I initially outlined the subjects for this book and gave them titles, I'd entitled this chapter "Fairy Rings and Other Things," because this section focuses on those many oddities we come across in life and how human curiosity draws us to them like moths to a flame. And how that flame can end up causing our demise. Yet I didn't keep the first draft title. I changed it to "The Humming" because that was so much more apropos. You see, curiosity is so deeply ingrained in the nature of humans that it's like a constant, thrumming vibration within. It's the frequency that makes people restless when they can't figure something out. It's what causes frustration when a solution to a problem remains elusive. It's our dynamic drive to seek out and to know.

We all have some measure of this "need to know." Curiosity is one of our stronger impulses. If it weren't, those tabloids stacked at the grocery store checkout would be out of business in a week's time. Their oftentimes preposterous headlines are purposely geared to catch the eye, hook the human curiosity, and reel in the price of the paper.

What I find interesting about this fascination with obviously incredible stories is the fact that most folks subconsciously know they're being taken for a ride, yet they still enjoy the thrill of it. I'm saying that people's curiosity is even sparked by the headlines they already know are untrue. People's curiosity gets the best of them every time and then, after reading the articles, they feel rather foolish for having paid out good money to read such tall tales. But next time they're in that grocery line, these same people let their eyes be magnetically drawn to the new headline.

Addiction. Is the human draw to the fantastic and outlandish an addiction? I believe it is for some. But for most I think the interest is more in line with amusement, entertainment, and fuel for conversation. We all enjoy a good laugh now and again–we all could use weekly doses of humor. Sometimes the tabloids simply offer a fun diversion.

The tabloids represent the extreme end of the concept of human curiosity. What's more subtle is our quest for answers to those enigmatic parts of our own lives. When a mother can't understand the unwise life decisions her daughter or son makes, she spends her days trying to identify where she went wrong in teaching that child to look at situations in a rational and logical manner before making a decision. When a father is told by his son that he doesn't want to make a career in the family business and instead wants to be a mechanic or an interior designer, the father searches for the answers that'll explain his son's lack of desire to follow in his footsteps. When my own life suddenly turned upside down and what had been routine normalcy became constant unpredictability, I wracked my brain trying to figure out what happened.

People quest for many types of truths. They want to discover why they're here, what their primary purpose for being here is. Folks go to all manner of extremes as their personal searches take on the form of an obsession.

Some New Agers will spend their entire life savings running from one popular guru to another up-and-coming channeler in an effort to gain the answers or perhaps to have some mystical aura rub off on them. Some folks will attend séances given by every psychic in the city in an effort to hear from a deceased loved one. Without their realizing how consumed they are by this pursuit of answers, their quests become overwhelming forces in their lives and they don't even notice what others around them have observed–that they've become neurotic.

Curiosity. Curiosity and the quest for answers is inherent. So how can it be bad if it's an innate human quality? Well, I'm not saying that all of these quests are bad. What I'm saying is that we as intellectual beings have to utilize those qualities of rationality and reason when choosing which answers to pursue. This is so because many quests preclude living.

Most of history's discoveries and advancements have been the results of some curious individual's quest for an answer. For example, Isaac Newton's observation of an apple falling from a tree made him ask, "Why did that apple fall?" His quest for the answer to that question led him to the discovery of gravity.

Those of us who are not scientifically involved still have our own quests for answers that stem from our specific relationships, beliefs, interests, philosophies, causes, and even sets of ethics and morals. Yet many times those answers will not be the end-all destinations we'd hoped they would be. Sometimes those answers we finally gain leave us wanting. They're not the fulfilling goals we'd envisioned. Why not? Why wouldn't they turn out to be the golden rings we reached for time and time again and finally grasped? It's because the answers we find aren't always those we want or expect. It's because sometimes the answer to one quest can be a door that opens up to expose a whole vista of fresh questions.

Calling oneself a seeker is okay, but the wise seeker keeps mental focus on one quest at a time rather than becoming fragmented with multiple goals. I've seen this fragmenting happen over and over again, especially when one's quest (or quests) has been given undue priority. When that happens the quest is no longer a quest; it becomes an obsession, which precludes involvement with all other aspects of life. When we pursue our questions in a healthy manner, we don't forsake any one of our daily responsibilities for some personal goal. What we do is integrate responsibilities with our personal interests. Balance. We maintain a balanced life.

Looking for answers to the questions we have and the experiential curiosities we come across is natural. The answers may be just as natural. This is a simple statement that's loaded with dynamic components. *The answers may be just as natural.* Take a minute or two to think about what that statement means.

So many times we enter into quests to unveil some mysterious or esoteric element of life. Maybe we pursue a question for the purpose of achieving public recognition or personal gain. Perhaps other searches are done for ego-stroking reasons. And, as I've witnessed, some have been entered into in order to experience alleged mystical events.

But nature is as nature does. I've said that before and I can't say it enough. Those folks who're seeking after the mystical, mysterious, and esoteric are going to be gravely disappointed when they reach the end of their quest and find the natural workings of nature at work. Nature is as nature does. It's natural. Its qualities, attributes, and behavior are all natural. What confounds people into believing these natural workings are mysterious or mystical is their ignorance or denial of nature's true beingness. Their lack of understanding reverts their intelligence back to that of a caveman, who thinks the fire was sent as a personal gift from the gods. Understanding the workings of nature does not make one a celebrated mystic. It merely means a person understands nature. Do you see where I'm going with this? I hope so. Because if you don't you'll continue as a seeker of nothing more than what is natural but you'll be thinking you're chasing after some quintessential, mystical secret to life.

It's good to question. It's also good to want to know the answers to puzzlements in your life. Yet most puzzlements don't need to be solved in order to be understood or accepted. We can spend far too much time missing out on enjoying our blessings while keeping our eyes glued fast on some glorified quest. It mesmerizes us so completely that we never feel the warmth of the sun on our faces, we never stop to admire a particularly striking sunset, we never really hear what our children are saying, or what our mate is telling us about her or his day. Quests for answers can become full-time preoccupations of the mind. They can dull one's emotional sensitivity and consume so many hours of the day that one will wonder where the time went.

These are not exaggerated scenarios. I've received letters from correspondents who want to leave their spouses and children in order to "find my truth" or "be a seeker on my special quest." I've watched people walk away from their life responsibilities to sit at the feet of some self-proclaimed guru. I've seen folks throw their lives away while believing that their quests are unique and sacred. *The honest and responsible living of one's daily life is a quest in itself.* That fact holds more sacredness than any mystical quest one can claim to have.

Are answers really more important than gaining an acceptance of What Is? And if those answers that one believes are going to be highly esoteric or mystical are actually nothing more than nature being natural, what has been gained by forsaking all else to learn that?

I hear the Humming and feel the sensation of it coursing up through my bare feet. I have an idea what is causing it, but I don't let it consume my thoughts. I just accept it as being a facet of nature.

Those dancing lights that accompany me on some night walks through the woods give me joy and companionship. That's more than enough for me. Why would I smother that joy with wondering curiosity?

Those crows. Mmm, what a sight they were. The awe that welled within me was such a happy and satisfying feeling that I look back and feel grateful for the birds' visit on my birthday morning. That's it. No hours of hard thinking. No days of deep contemplation or picking it apart with analysis that just spoils the experience.

That diminutive nature being I spied in the park. What about that little naked woman? I *know* what my eyes *saw* that day. The experience gave me all the verification I would ever need on the subject of nature beings, so why quest for more?

The wolves. I'm convinced that the ones Sally and I saw were the manifestations of some type of guardian that'd come during the most threatening time in my life. I'm deeply appreciative, for their presence gave me much comfort. To want to know more would, to my way of thinking, be highly disrespectful.

The South Fork mutilated deer. Ahh, I think it's rather obvious why I'd not wish to pursue that one. Just the fact that it was removed so quickly makes me want to keep my distance from delving further into that one. Perhaps it was the graceful hand of Providence that inspired me to keep my camera at home.

The two pair of owls. No questions roll around in my mind about that one. We were thrilled with their presence and felt blessed by their welcoming communion. To look for them to reappear would be to live in expectation rather than be alert to the new wonders that will appear. What transpired was a beautiful event. We'll always treasure the memory.

The three floating orbs in the night. We have no questions regarding those. They appeared and vanished just as suddenly. We don't spend time looking out our cabin windows for them every night. We don't expect them to come again. Perhaps it was an isolated incident, perhaps it'll happen again sometime. Whatever.

Whatever . . . Nature is as nature does. And to quest for an answer greater than that wise understanding is to waste a life trying to stand on a cloud.

glittering gold—understanding value

MANY YEARS AGO MY IMMEDIATE FAMILY AND a couple of dear members of our extended family lived together for six months in a small Colorado mountain town called Leadville. To this day Leadville has the distinction of being the highest-elevation incorporated city in the United States. In the 1800s many miners walked away from its silver mines as millionaires. There are now only one or two working mines left, and just a few of the current residents are hard rock miners. Most folks there make their living at the nearby ski resorts in Copper Mountain and Vail.

Just on the outskirts of the town there is a beautiful alpine body of water called Turquoise Lake. We were fortunate enough to live in a modest rental house on one of the highest hills of the city. The place overlooked the whole of the town and, from the generous bank of kitchen windows, we could see the lake just beyond the school complex. Several of the photographs I took for my pictorial book, *Whispered Wisdom,* were of this body of water.

Leadville is a chilly place to live in during the winter, but during the summer months we'd frequently take leisurely drives along the only road that circled the lake. At the halfway point of this drive, we'd discovered an unmarked treasure that turned out to be our favorite spot to spend an afternoon. The area we came to love was walking distance from the road, but it was not a lakeside location, as one might expect. It was on the western side of the high drive circumnavigating the lake and was easy for passing drivers to miss because there was nothing outstanding about it from the road. Unless, of course, one thinks a slightly wider shoulder area large enough to accommodate three vehicles is worth exploration.

It was our neighbor Mary who told us about the beauty of this much overlooked place. She was also the real estate agent who rented the house to us. With her directions we found the spot and investigated. Upon getting out of the car, we could immediately hear a stream running down the mountainside. The first obstacles we encountered were the rocks we had to step across to avoid being ankle-deep in icy water. Once those were maneuvered, a little-used trail lead us alongside the stream, which tumbled and exploded over large boulders.

The former rippling stream sounds became a roar as we approached a substantial wooden bridge spanning white water. This is the type of bridge that invites one to tarry and watch the torrent of water beneath. Both the log bridge and the dense surrounding of towering evergreens growing from banks carpeted with thick, green moss seemed to transport us onto the page of an elaborately illustrated children's picture book depicting a magical enchanted forest. It was one of those rare and wonderful places on the planet where those claiming to be confirmed skeptics regarding the existence of little nature sprites and winged fairies might find themselves experiencing a twinge of belief.

After traversing the bridge, we were led into an expanse of wide meadow surrounded by century-old pines and firs. On the east side of this meadow was a different type of stream, a shallow one that was flat and wide. It was more like a meandering pond that was so shallow we could roll up our pant legs and wade in the water, which only reached our ankles. This place was all our friend told us it would be. This was our vision of the ideal mountain picnic place. Sunshine poured down on the meadow clearing heavily scented with the fragrance of wildflowers. The sunrays beaming down upon the streambed dazzled the eye with countless glints of color . . . the color of gold.

In our bare feet we gently walked upon that wavering magic carpet of yellow sequins and, upon leaving the glistening waters, the soles of our feet were coated with flecks of gold. We were suddenly wearing the sandals of a goddess and leaving a path of radiant footprints across the mossy bank.

Ahh, but I'm talking about *nature's* precious golden treasures, not the kind of gold that drives men crazy with greedy dreams of material wealth and the alleged power it brings. Those sandals of the goddess were woven out of the golden fibers of pyrite. So fragile. So much more beautiful than true gold, for pyrite sparkles and glistens while real gold gives off only a dull shine. That beautiful pyrite has been called fool's gold, because so many gold seekers have mistaken it for true gold. Yet as I sat streamside admiring the gold sparkles gently drifting about with the flowing current, the thought crossed my mind that people have it all backwards. It's the dull, true gold that makes fools of folks. It's the shimmering pyrite that instills a deep appreciation of our world's natural beauty. It's the lustrous radiance of nature's simplicity reflecting the beauty of the *simple* things in life that far outshines the lackluster qualities of life's complexity caused by greed and materialism. Watching the glimmering pyrite in the streambed, its flakes glowing like celestial bodies slowly moving through the vast cosmos, made me feel rich with spiritual fulfillment. And never have I found myself wishing that the glittering flecks were real gold dust.

How is it that the golden-colored particles that sparkle and wink with the touch of a sunray can be more valuable than the golden-colored particles that are dull yet yield material wealth? That's the question the Old Woman of the Woods places before us when She opens the fingers of Her aged hand and lets Her precious flecks of pyrite sift through them to fall upon the ground like grains of sand.

Leadville is not the only place I've enjoyed a profusion of pyrite. It also exists on the mountain where I live. My driveway sparkles with pyrite. When I'm digging around in the flower garden, pyrite is everywhere. Our dogs come in from the yard with specks of it glinting off the pads of their paws. It's tracked into the cabin, leaving the carpet with golden highlights as if someone had sprinkled glitter about. I've even seen it glinting off bird wings. Everywhere. Everywhere, the glint of gold. The simple beauty of our world is so incredible. It's so awesome that the wealth of joy it fills me with leaves me speechless. All I can do is just . . . sigh.

Nature is so full of untold riches.

So too are our lives.

Yet people laboriously toil, digging for the dull elements that they think are going to turn their lives into paradise-like existences of ease with no wants, no needs. Folks think irrationally when they believe wealth, status, control, and the like are synonymous with acquired power. With such a philosophy people are never truly grounded in reality. These folks have a fundamentally twisted or fragmented idea of true value. These are the folks who have lost their emotional sensitivity to life. These are the folks who don't stop to smell the wildflowers growing on the roadside. These are the ones who will snicker at the suggestion of taking the time to admire a fiery sunset. And these are those who become ruthless, stepping on the shoulders of others to climb the corporate or social ladder. Their sensitivity becomes drowned beneath the weight of their own egos and distorted perception of value. Worth suddenly carries a whole new set of parameters.

It seems to me that it'd be really easy to devise a test that would effectively evaluate an individual's perception of value. Whether one found spectacular beauty in the streambed's glittering pyrite or whether one cursed it for not being real gold. When this one question is answered, a person's materialistic tendencies would be made clear. The test would have other questions that would similarly indicate the level of personal integrity, ethical principles, and moral fiber. It would be an unequivocal test that accurately revealed one's measures of trustworthiness, loyalty, honesty, veracity, and honor. Most important, it would reflect one's level of self-absorption. This final element is most important, because a totally self-absorbed individual will have a strong tendency toward ruthless behavior. Isn't it interesting what one little test could expose about a person's personality, goals, and psychological composition?

The wisdom ways of the Old Woman of the Woods are not highly esoteric, nor are they full of complexities beyond our understanding. For Her to place the sparkling pyrite so generously at our feet was no mistake. For Her to bury the true, dull gold deep underground so that we'd have to get past the surface pyrite and then work to dig up that gold was not happenstance. She's trying to convey to us that we have to first notice, then appreciate the simple things in life that we've all been blessed with. We have to first perceive these simple beauties that generously surround us and then show gratitude for them.

Simplicity. Life is so full of generously offered gifts that have the potential for uplifting us and changing our worldview. However, with the goal of "going for the gold" ingrained as the sole mind-set of our society, all the simple beauties go unnoticed and, consequently, unappreciated as we miss out on their bountiful benefits.

The greatest distortion of value is generated from a false perception of oneself. When the self is prioritized above all else, one's own perception cripples the ability to relate effectively to reality. That sounds pretty serious. And that's exactly what it is . . . extremely serious business. And those involved in this business have several names, one of which is Gold Digger.

I've known a few gold diggers in my life. Each came with a different agenda. Although each agenda's outward characteristics proved to be different, all these gold diggers had the same motive. Everything in their lives they manipulated for the eventual benefit of self.

One individual entered into marriage with the sole intention of inheriting his in-laws' money. The trouble was that this gold digger had made a wrong assumption: His belief that his in-laws were wealthy was incorrect. When he learned of the mistake, this man immediately divorced his wife.

Another individual I knew sacrificed his integrity for the prospect of gaining an inheritance from an individual who physically and mentally abused his wife and children. This self-centered person was so focused on getting some money down the line that he overlooked the abuse of the wealthy individual. Integrity was smothered with a blanket of denial. Cruel behavior was effectively covered over with visions of money piles. Integrity was drowned by greed.

When people hear the word *value,* they almost always get a mental visual of paper money, coins, stocks, real estate in a prestigious residential area or business district, a BMW, a Ming dynasty vase, the Hope diamond, a yacht, et cetera. These are all objects, touchable objects that have to be acquired or possessed. They're material possessions meant to be held or hidden, publicly displayed or sequestered away. Rarely do folks think of value in terms of character qualities, such as integrity. Yet integrity is the essential Who of our personal beingness. And now the Old Woman of the Woods is wearing a big smile, because we've finally come to the core moral of this comparison between Her sparkling pyrite and the dull shine of her true gold.

True value is the highest attribute of the untouchable aspects in life. These priceless aspects are untouchable because they are not objects to be bought and sold, exchanged or stolen. They are not three-dimensional, nor do they have shape or form. True value isn't found in a newly uncovered Egyptian queen's burial tomb. True value isn't shaped in the irregular configuration of a dull nugget of gold plucked out of the calm area of a rushing stream. True value isn't an inheritance or a lottery windfall. True value cannot be touched, or spent, or sequestered in a locked vault. True value is not material at all, it's spiritual . . . of the spirit . . . and is visible only through the expression of *positive* behaviors and *clear* perceptions of reality.

True value is in the inherent *beauty* of life rather than in its *material* worth. This is the truth that nature conveys through innumerable simple examples so obviously placed before our eyes to see and learn from throughout our daily lives. And so, what this analogy between the nature of Nature and the nature of human beings reveals is that the true *value* of human nature is in the expressed *behavioral* beauty of one's *inner* essence rather than any *exterior physical* characteristic.

The design of a book's dust jacket doesn't necessarily reflect the content of the text sandwiched within its wrap-around glossiness. You can't judge a book's worth based on its physical presentation–on the appearance of it. A dust jacket is just a dust jacket. A cover is just a cover. A *cover.* A cover that may or may not do justice to what can be found within. Granted, it's no secret that hundreds of books are purchased on the basis of cover appeal. Yet the fact that this is so says something about how people are automatically drawn to aesthetic presentation in life. The basic issue here is how folks prejudge elements of their reality by first sifting it through their own sets of "acceptable" physical characteristic parameters. This tendency leaves much to be desired in the way of gaining a fully rounded basis of knowledge.

For example, if someone makes an assumption about another individual based on her or his style of dress, ethnicity, or any other discriminatory element, how is that someone ever going to really get to *know* that other person? See what I mean? The issue of value in our society is so skewed, so shallow, that most folks live their entire lives floating on the surface without ever putting their heads in the water, much less diving in and seeing the wonders there are to discover and cherish within reality's spectacular depths.

Great works of literature are frequently disregarded out of hand just because their cover designs don't catch a person's eye and spark his or her intellectual curiosity. Life is not about cover appearances, life is about content . . . substance. That's where the true value is. If we shouldn't judge a book by its cover, then why are folks doing that with most aspects of their lives? They're making a cursory scan of the cover and, if they don't like what they see, they snub their noses as if they've been assaulted by some obnoxious odor.

The true worth of an individual is not reflected by skin color, by what church is attended, by whether real diamonds or cubic zirconium are worn. Why is it that someone carrying a Gucci handbag is generally perceived as being better than someone carrying a bag bought at a chain department store? You see? Even the preoccupation society has with labels gives clear evidence of this twisted view of value. Am I perceived differently when wearing an L.L.Bean flannel shirt than I am when wearing one of my home-sewn calico skirts? Probably. Personally, I could not care less about the assumptions people make when they see my choice of clothing, but the fact remains that folks have a tendency to form judgments of others based on their clothing style or other external characteristics.

Remember that little quiz I mentioned earlier? Let's see what a few more of its questions might be.

Have you ever experienced embarrassment (however slight) over introducing a physically unattractive friend to others?

What's more attractive to you when you're playing the field, a good personality or good looks?

If you're shopping with someone and he offers to pay the lunch tab, do you order the most expensive item on the menu or choose from those in the middle range?

Are you sometimes turned off or made uncomfortable by another's acts of unconditional goodness?

If asked whether you'd like to have a clothing gift certificate from Lands' End or Sears, which would you choose?

Which is more appealing in a man, his obvious appearance of machismo, masculine qualities or his gentleness?

If you had to choose between great wealth or fidelity in your mate, which would it be?

In your opinion, who possesses more worth in society, the woman with the high intelligence quotient who has several Ph.D.'s or the simple country woman with deep wisdom?

Have you ever hesitated to tell someone that you purchased something at a Big Kmart?

If your home burned to the ground and you lost every material possession, which item or items would you be most heartbroken over losing?

When seeking a home to purchase, would you look in the most upscale neighborhood you could afford or merely search for something you really like that fits your personality?

Do you perceive status and character differentiations between the person drinking a bottle of beer and the individual drinking a fine vintage wine?

Have you ever been reticent to express an opinion that differs from others'?

What characteristic is more important to you in your mate or significant other, social decorum or emotional sensitivity and its free expression?

Which attracts you more to a book: the cover, the title, or the subject matter?

Have you ever been attracted to a married individual?

What types of role models do you admire, the rich and famous or those who have made a measure of humanitarian difference in the world?

If you could be whoever you wanted, who would that be?

Have you ever been embarrassed because your house doesn't look like it came out of an illustration in a Martha Stewart magazine?

Have you ever apologized for your appearance?

Have you ever felt inferior when telling someone what you do for a living or where you work?

Have you ever been nice to someone thinking that by doing so you would gain something down the road?

If you had to choose between being gifted with a Ming vase or something your grandma made, which would it be?

When you've been out shopping with friends, have you ever refrained from buying something because you were fearful of hearing negative or sarcastic comments about the item?

In your opinion, which wields more power, vengeance or acceptance?

Do you get nervous or excited when in close proximity to a celebrity?

Which holds more worth, a well-rounded stock portfolio or a basement full of emergency supplies?

Do you judge a person's financial status by the type of vehicle she or he drives?

Are the high-minded book titles on your home bookshelves displayed more prominently than the frivolous ones?

If you could be given a large estate or a country farmhouse with acreage, which would you choose?

Have you ever purposely said things about yourself that you thought would make others admire you more?

Have you ever been reticent to express your desire to break away from family traditions?

Which brings you more joy, birdsong or opening a gift?

Well? How do you think you did? Few people could read those questions and not mentally answer them. And a few folks, catching the drift of the questions and sensing the "right" answers, may have responded with their self-image rather than honesty in mind. That doesn't really matter, though, does it? It doesn't really matter because the lying speaks for itself. It not only speaks–it shouts.

These questions are just a small sampling of the type of

query that has the ability to unwrap one's subconscious cloak of value perception. In case you couldn't see the connection between some of the questions and one's view of value, we'll take a closer look.

Have you ever experienced embarrassment (however slight) over introducing a physically unattractive friend to others?

If you honestly answered no to this question, then you understand the powerful value of true friendship. There should be no characteristic (physical or otherwise) about a friend that should cause you embarrassment or humiliation in the company of others. Mutual respect is a fundamental element that prolongs friendships into lasting relationships. The recognition and absolute acceptance of a friend's individuality, no matter how unconventional or idiosyncratic, is a sign of maturity and a commendable character trait. It exemplifies the fact that the value of being free to express oneself is a right, even in the face of how that expression is perceived by others.

What's more attractive to you when you're playing the field, a good personality or good looks?

This is obviously one of those questions that'd be easy to lie to yourself about, but remember, even lying to yourself is telling because you still know it's a lie by that little twinge of guilt that irritates your conscience like the itch of a mosquito bite. You know what your true responses are.

To be realistic, people are usually first drawn to the way someone looks. The personality isn't an immediately known factor. Yet this question is geared toward the time when the personality factor has become known. And if that personality proves to be undesirable, yet the relationship continues because your ego is inflated every time you're seen with this highly attractive individual, something serious is amiss in your perception of value. In essence, you're *using* this person to boost your self-image and attempting to raise the opinion others have of you based on the appearance of the people you're seen with. Dating someone for appearance alone is entirely self-serving. And there is not a mote of value if anything is done for self-serving reasons.

If you're shopping with someone and he offers to pay the lunch tab, do you order the most expensive item on the menu or choose from those in the middle range?

Clearly, the correct answer to this question is to choose from midline offerings. Otherwise you're taking advantage of another's generosity. But how does this question relate to one's perception of value?

Well, the value we're talking about here isn't the price of the prime rib or the burger, it's the singular issue of generosity and kindness, how one responds to gifts offered. Generosity, if offered without the expectation of any return for oneself, is a real treasure. The recognition of that treasure by others is a sign of wisdom. Conversely, to take advantage of that treasure is to adulterate its reciprocation with greed.

Are you sometimes turned off or made uncomfortable by another's acts of unconditional goodness?

If you answered yes to this query, it's an indication that you're feeling some form of guilt over not performing more of these acts yourself. Or that positive response could mean you don't recognize the high value of unconditional acts of goodness, you don't understand why people take the time or expend the effort to do all those little (or sometimes extensive) acts. After all, why go out of your way for someone if you don't absolutely have to? Huh? Those folks who lack this understanding may have a skewed attitude toward those who continually volunteer for others–a misconception that the acts are performed solely for ulterior motives. But if an act is truly unconditional, it is done with no thought of repayment. Some people cannot understand that idea–that an act can be truly unconditional, done with no thought of repayment. The concept isn't within their scope of understanding because the attitude is outside their realm of behavior.

I've witnessed people's jaded attitudes more often than I can mention. Who goes out of their way for others anymore? Isn't everyone too busy? Too preoccupied? Too overloaded with their own things to do? Well, the answer is a definitive no. Don't folks usually make the time for the things they want to do, to accomplish, to enjoy? Likewise, they can make the time to help others out. And plenty of them do. They do it without expecting so much as a thank-you in return. Unconditional goodness is one of the most valuable practices a human being can perform for another. Its worth is not short-lived, its benefits are extensive and far-reaching for the recipient . . . and the provider.

If asked whether you'd like to have a clothing gift certificate from Lands' End or Sears, which would you choose?

This question is clearly directed toward one's perception of value as related to labels and societal status symbols. I'll not be reluctant to state that making labels important is an incredibly shallow thing to do. I won't beat around the bush about saying that anyone who has to have only the alleged higher-end clothing labels is a snob who is ignorant of real value.

There is no value in status symbols, because seeking after status is inconsequential when it comes to spiritual growth. I know folks who consider a gift a "good" gift if it has the right label attached. This perception isn't exclusive to clothing, either. Whether it's camping gear, cameras, or electronic equipment; whether it's furniture or the brand of house stain doesn't matter–the label is still important to them.

Granted, some brand names are inherently better made and of higher quality than others, but this question is directed toward people's association of value with the brand names that in their minds symbolize societal status. And that perception ties in with one's ego. But there is no prime seating reserved for ego in the arena of value.

Which is more appealing in a man, his obvious appearance of machismo, masculine qualities or his gentleness?

Male gentleness wins hands down over physical masculine qualities every time. That's not only my personal opinion, that's a fact of value. Physical characteristics are surface elements. Remember that concept of the book cover versus what's inside? Real value is getting past the cover. Real value is discovered only after one truly recognizes That Which Lies Within. And a man who is a true gentle man possesses far more worth than one who is attractive with all the traditionally perceived "manly" physical traits yet has no gentleness dwelling within. If you answered this question by picking the "attractive" choice, then your set of values is founded on elements that are less than skin deep.

If you had to choose between great wealth or fidelity in your mate, which would it be?

I can already hear many of you saying, "Both!" Well yeah, that'd be nice, but the real worth is in the fidelity; material wealth is only an ancillary benefit. Obviously, wealth will not bring happiness without the attendant fidelity. Fidelity is the sealing bond that keeps the relationship together through thick and thin, regardless of financial state. Those who marry for money are gold diggers who will sacrifice all for the wealth and social status it brings.

In your opinion, who possesses more worth in society, the woman with the high intelligence quotient and several Ph.D.'s or the simple country woman with deep wisdom?

Your answer to this question is associated with your perception of value as related to education. In some circles, education is in a class of its own in how an individual is perceived. If someone never went to college, there are folks who relegate that someone to a lower class. With this erring attitude, pity the person who never finished high school!

The trouble with this perception of value is that people are equating intelligence with wisdom. But in reality intelligence (no matter how great) is worthless without attained and applied wisdom to go along with it.

I've known many people who had Mensa-level IQs yet had no wisdom, no vision, and absolutely no common sense. The thought processes that relied upon simple logic were grossly lacking. So what good were their fancy degrees? What real worth was their education other than the gathering of extensive information? For highly intelligent people to lack wisdom, logic, rationality, and plain common sense is mind-boggling to me. Their intelligence becomes meaningless when applied to solving life's problems and addressing its complexities.

Those possessing clear rationality, simple logic, common sense, and wisdom are far more valuable assets to society than those displaying only college degrees and no wisdom. In my opinion, the little old wrinkled woman who lives down in one of the deep hollows of southern Missouri and is known for her great wisdom is far more valuable to her neighbors than someone with high intelligence who has no clue as to what the wise woman is talking about. Formal education is fine. It's well and good, but only if it's married to wisdom.

Have you ever hesitated to tell someone that you purchased something at a Big Kmart?

If you answered yes, then you put value on store names and are intimidated by the opinions of others. Both are contrived and illusionary values tied to one's self-esteem as seen in the superficial image reflected back from the mirrors of others. Why? Doing things like this only covers up your true beingness, which, it seems, you're somehow embarrassed of. If you prefer to shop at places like Big Kmart and Wal-Mart, so what? Perhaps your reason for going to these stores is limited finances, and that too is a somewhat humiliating reality for you. As long as you're working to support yourself, doesn't that fact hold value enough for you? You do what you can and, if that means shopping at the less expensive stores, then so what? You see, your *worth*–your character value–is in the *working* you do to make ends meet. It's not in *where* you shop to make that goal a success.

Now let's look at the other end of this question's conceptual basis. If others make comments that embarrass you about where you do your shopping, who are the ones with the real character flaws? First of all, it's unkind to make such statements or insinuations to others. The *source* has to be considered. Those who humiliate others or make them feel inferior in any way don't deserve the time of day from you. To place worth on their words is to misunderstand character values and overvalue others' opinions. The value of your own hardworking beingness far outweighs the thoughtless crudeness of someone whose perception of value is entangled in labels and social status symbols.

If your home burned to the ground and you lost every material possession, which item or items would you be most heartbroken over losing?

It doesn't take a philosopher to see where this question is headed, yet we're still shooting for complete honesty here, and you have to remember that or else you'll only succeed in fooling yourself.

The answer to this question shouldn't be a quick one. I agree that many material possessions would be greatly missed. They may be one-of-a-kind items. Some may be family heirlooms. A few may carry great monetary value. All of them need to be considered before coming to a conclusive answer. Think this one through for a moment.

Now, to what have you assigned the greatest value?

Human life should've been perched at the pinnacle of your list. Second in priority should've been the lives of your beloved pets. All else is just stuff. I repeat, all else is just so much material stuff.

We don't stop to think about all the stuff we stuff into our homes. Yes, we do think it all has value to us or we wouldn't have put it there. Yet the fact that it's all still just so much stuff is the point of reasoning out its value here. Life doesn't stop at losing one's stuff. Life goes on as one begins anew.

I have a cabin full of stuff, too. I have possessions that are irreplaceable. I have a basement full of boxes packed with my books that are signed first editions. Their covers have never been cracked, and they are classified as mint condition. I have my handwritten journals. And the very special notebook in which *Spirit Song* and *Phoenix Rising* were written, in the handwriting of someone other than myself.

Family photo albums.

My extensive collection of nature sprite figurines.

Pottery handmade by a very special, aged American Indian woman.

Signed first editions by deceased famous authors.

Special gifts from my readers and friends.

Just the sight of all the knotty pine paneling that Sally and I worked so hard and long to install on all the interior walls burning up in a fire would be terribly sad.

Sure, I'd feel bad about watching all of those things burn to a crisp, yet I know that I would not grieve over their loss because, in reality, it's still all just stuff. As long as I got all the people and pets out of the burning cabin, I'd feel like the most blessed person on the planet and I'd be as happy as happy gets.

Life. Always, the value of life over the value of stuff. There's no contest.

When seeking a home to purchase, would you look in the most upscale neighborhood you could afford or merely search for something you really like that fits your personality?

The type of value this question reflects is, once again, perception of social status and the worth it carries.

If you found the perfect home, your dream home, but it wasn't quite in the "right" area of town, why wouldn't you still purchase it? By discarding your dream home, you'd have compromised your integrity. And that compromise would have been generated by a misplaced perception of value. And the value I'm talking about is being true to oneself instead of attempting to be true to the opinions of peers. Making the latter choice proves that you allowed status to pressure you into a less desirable choice. You must value all facets of your path, those unique life elements that complement your own vibrations. Most important, you must *know* yourself enough to *like* that self and be completely comfortable with that image of beingness.

What does choosing the upscale house bring you if you still find yourself thinking of the other house? Choices. So many choices that don't have to be nearly as difficult as people make them if they'd only understand the true value of things. Being true to oneself carries far greater value than attempting to be true to someone else's opinion or definition of value.

Do you perceive status and character differentiations between the person drinking a bottle of beer and the individual drinking a fine vintage wine?

Clearly, this type of query deals with the perception of value folks can have based on superficial choices.

Fine wines, especially those exorbitantly priced brands, are often thought to be reserved for the highest class of people. Ta-ta. By contrast, beer is considered to be for those beer-bellied, football-watching, blue-collar folks who have no class. Burp. Isn't this the general perception society has taken on?

Yet who is to say that that CEO in the Brooks Brothers suit and vest who drank the fine wine at the corporate dinner didn't go straight home afterward, open up a cold bottle of beer, and lounge in his boxers in front of the television watching a football game, frequently belching his pleasure?

Who is to say that the slovenly dressed guy in the lounge who's downing one beer after the other and getting louder and more repulsive by the minute isn't one of the city's most powerful and celebrated attorneys?

Making judgments of value based on outward appearances or behavior in this way is not showing wisdom. The commonly accepted theory that first impressions are everything is flawed, because these first impressions can frequently be completely erroneous. And we do others a great disservice by adhering to a preconception that's clearly built on a faulty foundation.

Have you ever been reticent to express an opinion that differs from others'?

I already know that many of you will have answered yes to this question, because you're fearful of being different and experiencing some form of sarcasm or humiliation as a result of that uniquely voiced variance.

If you deem another's opinion valuable, why isn't yours a likewise valuable and valid opinion? See what I mean? This returns to the idea that you don't view your intelligence, logic, or ideas as having as much worth and weight as others'. Why not, I ask? Perhaps you feel intellectually inferior because you've had no higher education and *they* finished college. Maybe you think others will ridicule your statement as ignorant or silly. Yet how will you ever begin being true to yourself if you don't feel that you can freely voice your opinions–no matter how unique they are–in the presence of others who may not agree with them?

You are what you think. To cover up those thoughts with conformity is a crime against self. It's being dishonest, not only in the presence of others but with yourself. Honesty is a far more cherished treasure than wearing a false face in order to be accepted by the majority.

What characteristic is more important to you in your mate or significant other, social decorum or emotional sensitivity and its free expression?

This may sound like an extremely odd question, but I assure you, it's germane to the issue of the perception of true value. When there's a choice between social decorum and outward expressions of emotional sensitivity, there's no contest. One tenaciously clings to the trellis of societal judgment while the other clings to nothing outside the freedom to express oneself through pure emotion. Again, no contest.

Social decorum has its place, of course, but not when its sacrifice is free expression of one's sensitivity. I can recall many times when I was married that I reached for my mate's hand in public and he declined to make a reciprocal motion. Instead, I received a look of admonishment that implied I wasn't being "proper." Proper? Come on, all I wanted to do was to express my feelings of closeness to him. Why should I care if others saw that expressed emotion? I've observed people in crowds acting the same way, and I shake my head to witness it. Why shouldn't such emotions be expressed when the urge arises in public?

Again, this is one of the ways that people's behavior exemplifies how their priority is placed on the value of peer opinion rather than their own impulses, instincts, and attitudes. This priority is falsely placed above free expression. It's directly related to the ego. The individual who buries his or her own expression does not wish to be seen doing anything he or she deems socially unacceptable.

Expressing one's love is accomplished in many ways. Smothering those expressions does far more damage than committing an alleged crime against social decorum.

Which attracts you more to a book: the cover, the title, or the subject matter?

A book's cover design and its title can be misleading. They can both be unattractive and unappealing. Yet isn't a book purchased for what may be found on all the pages inside? Subject matter is the meat between the slices of bread–the real substance you're looking to be satisfied by. Good grief, some of the cover designs on books on my bookshelf are, in my opinion, atrocious. So are some of the titles, which have no connection to the books' essential content. Yet I keep no book that doesn't prove to have some form of intellectual value. Interesting subject matter is what I look for when perusing a bookstore or book catalog. I go for the substance.

Substance. This concept can be applied to every aspect of life. Substance of content is where the true value and worth can be found, not upon the surfaces or in the name, not in ethnicity or choice of political party. The substance of an individual is not reflected in what she drinks or which store he shops at. Neither mode of dress nor a tendency to be outspoken (or shyly quiet) defines the true content of a person's core character and personality. Value is found in the inner substance, not in the many forms of external appearances that are, more often than not, misleading.

Remember, substance carries the value, superficiality holds none.

Have you ever been attracted to a married individual?

This may seem like an unrelated question, but it's not. This issue is relevant to the subject of value as it's associated with personal integrity.

The fact that an individual wears a wedding band, or even if the ring's hidden but you're aware she or he is married, means that that person is off limits for any romantic involvement. That's always been a given, hasn't it? Regardless, it would appear that many choose to ignore that "given" or slip into denial of it. And personal integrity goes out the window along with fidelity because "we want to do what we want to do!" Me, me, me, and damn the integrity torpedoes.

Sensitivity to the suffering of the married individual's mate is viewed as inconsequential when weighed against pursuit of the desired individual. It's no secret how rampant infidelity has become in our society. The discovered marital indiscretions of public figures (mostly married men, by the way), are on the nightly newscasts. Women by the hundreds are exacerbating the behavior because they've participated in such infidelity.

Those involved in relationships of infidelity and those who encourage them don't really think much of themselves. These people give little consideration to their integrity. Yet without integrity there's no quality substance to a person. Such people's perception of value drops down into their raging hormones instead of remaining evenly dispersed from the central core of their intelligence, which inherently *knows* the difference between right and wrong behavior.

What types of role models do you admire, the rich and famous or those who have made a humanitarian difference in the world?

The correct answer to this one is fairly obvious, but the question still needs to be answered honestly in order to evaluate accurately your perception of value.

Those who are rich and famous receive a great deal more publicity and notoriety than people who quietly go about doing works of unconditional goodness. We've heard a lot about Mother Teresa, yet there are hundreds of ordinary people in the world who daily practice selfless humanitarian acts without wanting any recognition for them. And this is exactly how it should be if those acts are performed in an unconditional manner.

Media folks give their viewers and listeners what they want in order to maintain and raise their ratings. This is why the kindly woman who lives down the country road and devotes her day to driving senior citizens around never gets on the newscasts. Yet the rich and famous folks who do acts of goodness (even one) get vast coverage and public praise.

Go figure.

Unconditional goodness carries the true value.

If you could be whoever you wanted, who would that be?

The answer to this question reveals one's idea of value as it's related to status, popularity, wealth, power, et cetera. The response here speaks for itself. It will point to either an egotistical slant or a selfless one. I don't have to state which has more value because you already know. The best scenario is that, if given the choice, you'd still want to be *you.*

Have you ever been embarrassed because your house doesn't look like it came out of an illustration in a Martha Stewart magazine?

If you answered yes, then you're doing that hiding your unique beingness thing. My first question to you would be this: Why would you (and so many others) want your home to look like someone *else's* concept of an ideal home? Where's the personalized character of your little nest if it's made to look like the expression of another? Each person's home should reflect that individual's personality in what it contains and how it's decorated. The contents and presentation of a home give off a specific aura associated with the owner. And to apologize for not creating a mirror image of someone else's character is almost shameful.

Feeling free enough to express your individuality through your home decor shows independence. And independence has value. It speaks of one's right to throw conformity out the window and be oneself.

Have you ever apologized for your appearance?

Maybe you've been in the middle of a gardening or construction project, had to run out to the hardware store for more supplies, and felt embarrassed to be wearing soiled or torn work clothes. Feeling this way, you just had to explain your appearance to complete strangers. But why? I think it was probably obvious to everyone seeing you that you were in the middle of a project.

Some folks just automatically apologize for how they look. There are several reasons for doing this. Looking for Mr. Good Compliment is one reason. People think if they give the impression that they don't look good, folks will say, "Oh no, you look great!" Well, I for one would like to know what the value of that compliment was if subterfuge was applied to elicit it. Some people apologize for how they look because they really believe that their manner of dress doesn't measure up to society's standards. If what one is wearing is a bit on the unconventional side, one may feel the need to make excuses. Why?

We're back to appearances again. Insubstantial and trivial surface elements in life that hold no water. They have absolutely no value.

Have you ever felt inferior when telling someone what you do for a living or where you work?

I hope not, because society has a preoccupation with job types that is so twisted it belongs in a wrecking yard.

The same misperception associated with one's level of education applies to careers or types of employment. Late-night talk show hosts seem frequently to make demeaning jokes about those working at McDonald's, yet many a young person has received his or her first work experience there or used the job to help get through school.

Why does society perceive the occupation of a doctor, lawyer, or judge as more valuable than that of the sanitation workers who keep the city streets and residential neighborhoods free from trash? What would affect society more, a lawyers' strike or a sanitation workers' strike? Think about that. So maybe lawyers don't have unions, but you get the gist.

Wake up and smell the value. As long as people are gainfully employed and working hard at paying their bills, what does it matter what kind of job meets the goals of being a productive, self-sufficient individual? Oh, we humans can be a snobbish, judgmental lot that cause others untold anguish. This is because the perception of real value has been almost irretrievably lost.

Have you ever been nice to someone thinking that by doing so you would gain something down the road?

Sounds terribly self-centered, doesn't it? It is. In fact, there are even several commonly used expressions for this type of behavior, *sucking up* being just one of them.

There's no redeeming value in kindness if it has strings attached. And every one of those strings has a multitude of names associated with it. All the names are tied to one thing–ego. The ego is focused only on self. What will I get? How can I advance by doing that for this other person? I'll be liked better if I do this. I'll be more popular if I do that. Me, me, me.

Kindness with strings attached negates any value it might have had standing on its own.

If you had to choose between being gifted with a Ming vase or something your grandma made, which would it be?

I came up with really obvious questions, didn't I? Whether the intent is obvious or effectively sequestered to trick the test taker isn't the point. The point is understanding your own perception of value. In this case the subject is material value versus the value of emotional attachments. Choosing the vase denotes a materialistic tendency. Going for Grandma's hand-knitted sweater indicates an understanding of true worth. The former choice lacks sensitivity, the latter connotes a placement of greater worth on simplicity and emotional ties.

When you've been out shopping with friends, have you ever refrained from buying something because you were fearful of hearing negative or sarcastic comments about the item?

Here again we come across an example of how one views personal integrity when set against peer pressure or public opinion. Which comes out the winner? The one you think is the winner is the one you perceive as being more valuable.

There is no value in peer pressure, but there's a hell of a lot of worth in being confident in one's own convictions. Peer pressure is a highly manipulative force, to which many fall prey out of a lack of self-esteem and a reluctance to assert their individuality.

The value of individuality is priceless. There's no denying the fact that the pressure of one's peers, whether in youth or out in the adult world, can be intense, yet the key to being immune to that heat is to be comfortable in one's own skin–one's unique beingness. When one has this comfort, peer pressure becomes a nonentity.

With individuality comes a whole set of special characteristics inherent to each person. Within that set of characteristics are endless elements associated with choice, such as personal tastes in clothing, home furnishings, hobbies, interests, philosophies, et cetera. To deny any of these because of peer pressure is to deny the essential "who" of self. There is no value in doing that. The value lies in the joy of celebrating who you are and all the many facets of that beautiful individual, which shine like celestial bodies high in the cosmos on a moonless night.

In your opinion, which wields more power, vengeance or acceptance?

This question is so simple that it almost sounds like a trick. It's not.

I've frequently witnessed people thinking they're extremely clever when saying, "Don't get mad, get even." Jeez Louise, that's supposed to be clever? That's the best they can come up with in the way of wisdom? Vengeance? An eye for an eye? Back stabbing?

I've also observed a generalized dread of acceptance. People don't want to have to expend the effort to accept things they don't like. They don't want to have to shed their anger or smooth out their irritation over something (or someone). They can't let sleeping dogs lie. It's so much easier to rant around the house and rave at any friend who's handy. It's so much more fun to hold on to the tails of revenge. It's easier to remain angry than to be soothed by acceptance and get on with life.

Yet there's a good measure of grace in acceptance–especially in quiet acceptance. That quiet acceptance comes when you don't go around broadcasting the fact that you're accepting something as though you were a martyr. That noisy kind of acceptance carries no grace, and its value is greatly lessened because it ends up being the ego's self-serving ploy, which says, "Look at me, everyone. Look how I accept this terrible situation without complaining! Aren't I wonderful!" Wonderful my eye!

So if you answered this question with "acceptance," you also have to examine the manner of that acceptance in order to come to a clear understanding of whether it carries false value or true worth and well-earned grace.

Do you get nervous or excited when in close proximity to a celebrity?

We've all seen the phenomenon of the swooning girls attending an Elvis concert or a Beatles performance. Groupies. Young and impressionable people who easily succumb to infatuations with performers and film stars.

These are the types of individuals who initially come to mind for most people when reading this question, but these love–struck, youthful groupies are only the tip of the iceberg. Adult infatuations are evidenced by the widespread popularity of sports figures when they become spokespeople for everything from cereal and shoes to credit card companies and long–distance telephone providers. The A–list film stars are no different, and neither are their adult admirers.

Society raises these folks high above the general mass of humanity and calls them *celebrities.* However, celebrities go shopping just like you do. Celebrities who birth babies go into the same labor as all other mothers of the world do. They walk on the same sidewalks as you and drive on the same roads. They have to adhere to the same laws, and they are not immune to physical ills. So . . . what makes these folks so much more elevated in the public eye? Is it their appearance? Their wealth? Their popularity or social status? If it's any of these, we've come full circle back to that book–cover concept of surface aspects. It's like venerating the eggshell and ignoring the protein hidden within. Although the color, texture, and shape of the eggshells may vary, the egg inside each one is still the same substance.

Celebrities are still just people. They make mistakes in life just like you do. They have to make decisions the same way you do. They experience depression, sadness, moments of elation, and family problems–all just like you do. To get excited or nervous in close proximity to someone who does so many things the same way you do makes no sense. Human beings are human beings. Fame doesn't make one any better than those who aren't famous. That beautiful face of the film star can be seen on comparable women walking down the streets of Everytown, USA.

Getting nervous or excited over being close to a celebrity speaks volumes about how an individual values the beingness of self. That excitement and nervousness says, "I'm just a

Little Person in the presence of a Great Person, and I'm awed and humbled." Is that how you value your beautiful beingness? Is that all you think of yourself as a member of the human race? A Nobody standing next to a Somebody? Oh, come on, you can do better than that for yourself. You may not think those exact thoughts, yet your demeanor says the same thing, and you need to examine those self-defeating ideas more closely.

Which holds more worth, a well-rounded stock portfolio or a basement full of emergency supplies?

The response to this question indicates whether you're planning for a financial future or a provisional one. Some believe that they're the same thing, however, there are many future probabilities that could negate any financial investments one amasses. Accumulating a financial base that will be used to purchase provisional goods at a later date is a tremendous risk.

Purchasing the emergency supplies a little at a time as one can afford them is far wiser, because when the unexpected emergency situation does arise, money in the bank or tied up in investments won't be accessible.

So here we have two ways of planning for one's future. One in the form of monetary investments and the other in the form of immediate purchases. I think it's clear which one carries the greater value. A bird in the hand is worth far more than two in the bush. When you're hungry, a canned ham is worth more than a handful of dollar bills.

Do you judge a person's financial status by the type of vehicle she or he drives?

I'm not sure if this is a common practice, yet I've witnessed enough comments to cause me to think it is a frequent error in judgment.

I once worked as a secretary in a real estate firm. One of the top agents thought he had a solid handle on a prospective buyer's financial status by the type and age of the vehicle she or he drove up in. When I first heard him make a comment about that clever way to evaluate clients, I frowned; to me it sounded incredibly illogical. In addition, this agent had an extremely wealthy client who always drove up in an old, beat-up pickup and walked into the office wearing torn and dirty overalls. So? So where did this agent get his rationale from?

I drive an old GMC pickup that isn't even the same color all the way around its rusty body. To my way of thinking, there's nothing more useful to drive when living in the rugged mountain terrain that I do, especially when that old pickum-up has so many handy uses. Even if I were wealthy and could purchase any type of new vehicle I wanted, I'd still have at least one older, dependable four-wheel-drive pickup. My gosh, Sally and I would be snowbound all winter long if we didn't have some type of four-wheel-drive vehicle to get us up through the deep snow that blankets our long, twisting drive.

Anyway, just like with all other forms of outward appearances, the type of vehicle one drives in no way reflects one's core beingness or the true value of one's inherent self. Neither does it denote one's financial worth.

When answering a question such as this one, you also have to remember that vehicle types are frequently faddish—and fads directly relate to what is called a status symbol. Here again we return to the concept of following the crowd and falling victim to materialistic peer pressure. I remember a time when driving a Jeep Cherokee was the yuppie craze. Yuck. Not *yuck* to the vehicle per se, but *yuck* to the idea. It's yucky for two reasons: one is that a person is allowing the opinions of peers to dictate what type of vehicle he or she purchases, and the other is that an individual is forced to purchase something she or he may not even like very much just to be counted among those up-and-comers. What if you really loved the Toyota RAV4?

Peer intimidation.

Loss of individuality and the freedom to express the same.

Diminished integrity generated by a voluntary choice to counter one's preferences.

Society's overall view of what carries worth needs to be shifted to the truly important aspects in life instead of the, surface dressing that conceals the real qualities that make the differences in our world.

Are the high-minded book titles on your home bookshelves displayed more prominently than the frivolous ones?

This question deals with the intellectual value you perceive, not just intellectual value but that value as it's associated with the ego. Folks can fully appreciate the value of intelligence and the ongoing quest to expand one's knowledge base. Yet when that intelligence is utilized as a *tool* to feed the ego's appetite for *recognition,* then the value of that intelligence and the unrelenting questing to expand it are sullied. Are you following me on this?

Intelligence has great value, but not when it lacks its partner, wisdom. The quest for knowledge is a beautiful endeavor, yet using that quest to inflate one's ego turns it ugly and withered. Putting one's intelligence on display is a self-serving act. It's a psychological ploy not only to elicit compliments but also to use knowledge for self-aggrandizement and self-satisfaction. This quest robs that knowledge of true worth.

If you could be given a large estate or a country farmhouse with acreage, which would you choose?

There are at least three factors that directly affect one's response to this question.

The first are possible fragmented aspects of one's past-life experiences. By this I mean that an individual could've lived several lives on a farm and thereby possess a subconscious, karmic attraction to that type of environment. The same applies to the large estate. So if the answer to this question is generated from this innate factor of one's composite personality, then it would have nothing to do with a current perception of value.

The second factor that may sway one's answer is associated with current-life experiences. For example, perhaps you were raised on a large estate with servants and, upon reaching adulthood, saw the superficiality of that kind of lifestyle and wanted nothing more to do with it. This scenario quite naturally generates a strong desire to reject the estate and seek out its opposite–the farm.

Conversely, those who are raised in simplicity (even poverty), may have a strongly ingrained goal to break out of that cycle and swear that they're going to seek greater financial independence. If these individuals' past was lived in poverty, the goal to reach for the stars is commendable. Yet if these people were raised in a loving and simple environment where all needs (and some wants) were provided for, then the desire to seek better and more could be based on ego-generated factors. See the difference?

The third aspect behind an answer to this question is personality. There are those who perceive the large estate as a social statement. They believe that living in such a place will bring them admiration, respect, awe, and/or envy. Everyone should have a moderate level of self-esteem. An average measure of self-esteem is what enables us to be of help to others. If we didn't have a basic amount of self-esteem, we'd be going around in a melancholy mood or be too overwhelmed by our shadows of inadequacy to be any good to ourselves or others. You don't need to *love* yourself, but you do at least have to have the perception that the *you* of you is an okay person.

So, concerning the question at hand, any attempt to inflate one's self-image with the kind of property one owns involves being egotistical and self-absorbed. One who makes such a choice is in a maze that always leads back to self.

Have you ever purposely said things about yourself that you thought would make others admire you more?

Again, this question is connected to your self-perception. And here we're not talking about naturally healthy self-esteem but about self-absorption. This question is clearly related to the psychological mechanisms of generating an inflated perception of oneself in the minds and eyes of others. Ego again. And that behavior possesses no value whatsoever. Behavior that's self-serving is selfish, even if that behavior is in the form of acts that help others.

Have you ever been reticent to express your desire to break away from family traditions?

Here we have a question about individuality as it's related to family traditions. Yet the concept also includes mainstream traditional behavior–the accepted norms of the so-called establishment. Let me give just a few examples.

Family holiday celebrations. More times than not they seem to dig a groove of tradition that gets deeper each year. No variety allowed. Yet as family members reach adulthood, perhaps move away with careers and families of their own, they may want to spend a holiday in a different manner. If so, they're faced with the necessity of breaking with family tradition and hoping that their decision will not be met with anger, hurt, or misunderstanding. The meat of the issue is whether such people actually *voice* the desire to alter those family traditions. The possibility of being intimidated by negative or disappointed comments, the fear that family members will use psychological ploys to make them feel bad prevent many people from speaking up and acting on their wishes to change. Perhaps you are afraid your family may think that you don't love them anymore or that you're trying to create distance from them. Whatever the reasons, the value related to this question is personal integrity and independence. And the *confidence* in oneself to *assert* those important qualities *without* being intimidated, humiliated, or made to feel you're the worst person in the world for doing so is the important character trait here.

The psychological ploys people utilize to manipulate others are as endless as they are damaging. Understanding these is one of the keys to being able to overlook them. Those hurtful comments should never reach your own heart but rather should be processed through the intelligence and clear wisdom of your mind. This way you are spared emotional trauma and, most of all, guilt.

People, sometimes without even realizing it, cause much

pain with their inconsiderate and egotistical behavior. Yet the negative effects of these behaviors can be avoided if a person simply understands this tendency and maintains with strength his or her own integrity and convictions. After all, integrity and individuality are rights that every human being has the freedom to preserve with dignity. Never let others deny those rights to you through any means of manipulation.

Which brings you more joy, birdsong or opening a gift?

Your response to this question may depend on whether you're a nature person or not, but the fundamental premise isn't wholely contingent on that factor.

My choice of birdsong was merely an example of the simple things that are counted among the free and natural blessings folks often choose to ignore or consciously deny. Birdsong is something everyone is exposed to, as are most of the other simple things in life that have the potential to uplift our spirits. These don't come gaily wrapped with colorful bows on top. They don't come with these external and insignificant trappings because . . . they just are. In their own natural beingness, they just are what they are. These are the small but often most precious and beautiful gifts we could ever receive because they have the power to brighten our days and lift our moods like no store-bought gift. They are more lasting than those gifts wrapped and formally presented to us.

THE WISDOM THAT THE OLD WOMAN OF THE WOODS SHARES IN THE glinting pyrite on the streambed exemplifies the multitudes of beautiful gifts nature presents us with. They are meant to bring joy to our hearts. They have the true value of simplicity, honesty, naturalness of being, free expression, and integrity.

The material value of real gold is not presented in such a manner. Real gold is lackluster and dull. It's hidden beneath the splendorous twinkle of the simple gifts we were meant to notice and appreciate first. It's hidden so that one has to work to earn its *material* worth.

The sparkling, simple blessings that surround us and are free for the enjoyment give us value so great that it's beyond calculation. They're all around us. From the cheeriness of birdsong to the tiniest wildflower growing alone on a mountainside, these natural blessings are created to beautify our world and enrich our hearts and souls.

And those other natural values are found only *beneath* the beauty of life's precious and priceless qualities of simplicity.

This is wisdom few stop to consider.

Wisdom few recognize as worth considering. Yet life's true valuables are the untouchables:

The awe-inspiring sunset that looks like fire in the sky.

The newborn fawn attempting to stand on wobbly legs beside its mother.

A new species of bird visiting your feeder.

A cool breeze on a stifling summer's afternoon.

Valuable gifts that warm the heart and chase away the shadows of the mind and heart. Our world is full of them. No matter where we live, they surround us. And all it takes to see and feel them is to open your eyes and . . . welcome the wonder you find filling up your soul.

valley in the clouds—doubts and fears

THE ELEVATION OF OUR CABIN CAN READ ANYwhere between 9,820 and 9,980 feet, depending on the altimeter one uses. We're actually higher than the town of Cripple Creek, which, some tourists seem to think, is a city in the clouds. The view of it from the highway overlook makes me think of the city as the Machu Picchu of the United States.

The air is much thinner here than at lower elevations, and it's common to see visitors walking around Cripple Creek pulling their oxygen tanks behind them. This, therefore, is not the ideal vacation destination for those with heart or respiratory problems. One of the advantages of the high elevation that I'm especially grateful for is that no snakes wind their way up here. Snakes are okay but, well, personally, I'd just as soon have them stay where they feel most comfortable. Fleas. We don't seem to have fleas on our pets, either. Maybe fleas don't care for the thin air (or perhaps they have heart problems?). At any rate, the veterinarians here 'bouts rarely see any sign of fleas on the animals they care for. Also, heartworms aren't seen here unless a pet is transported from a lower elevation, where there is an abundance of mosquitoes carrying the disease.

The one aspect of living this high up that amazed me most when I first moved here was the ghostly, white mists that would mysteriously weave their way through the forests and across the roadways. They were not what I thought they were. I called them fog and was quickly corrected. I was seeing clouds. The clouds would frequently lower themselves to altitudes of 6,000 feet and blanket entire high-country towns.

Sometimes when driving from a high elevation to a lower one, you can see the bank of clouds lying like a blanket of billowing cotton over the landscape below you, or its whiteness will be following the twisting, deep canyons of a mountain pass as though it were using the highway to make its way up back into the sky. Sometimes, when one is looking down, these banks of clouds appear so thick that they look like one big, fluffy feather bed someone has tossed over the land.

The blanket of clouds that visits our own remote valley is as dense as this from time to time. You can always see it coming in. The far ridge tries to snag it to a halt but never succeeds. The opaque cloud bank creeps forward.

First the farthest ridge of Quartz Mountain is obscured from view.

Then the ridge directly across the valley from us is hidden.

The rolling and tumbling curtain silently lowers itself into the valley floor.

It creeps closer and closer, magically making everything behind it vanish.

Little by little, the tall aspen, spruce, and pine trees in front of the cabin disappear as the spectral white entity approaches. Then absolutely nothing can be seen out the window but . . . clouds. The cabin becomes entirely engulfed in clouds. A cabin in the clouds. That's exactly what it is. And that's when one can honestly say that she's danced in the clouds. What a wonder!

However, another amazing part of this event is that, if I get in the truck and drive up to the road and then toward Cripple Creek, the sun may be brightly shining through a cobalt blue sky, the atmosphere all around as clear as crystal. The cloud bank is never everywhere at once. It drifts along on the frivolous whims of the air currents, moseying over mountaintop and valley alike.

This spectral cloud on the move is not only physically interesting and pleasing to the eye but also philosophically interesting and pleasing to the analytical mind. The ambling cloud blanket has something to convey to those who will spend a few moments contemplating its deeper message. The Old Woman of the Woods is speaking to us with the bank of clouds, which, like a sorceress's wand, makes reality vanish (shift) for a short span of time.

As one who looks under philosophical rugs and peers behind curiosities, I've given deep thought to this intriguing and provocative phenomenon. The eerie sensation I have when these cloud curtains slowly approach and engulf me and my cabin is what prompted my musings.

Watching the clouds' advance, I know that there's nothing I can do to stop it. I can see that they're moving toward me and will soon overtake my beingness. They will soon obliterate all visuals around me, and I'll be left without a single point of familiar reference. And that gives me the oddest sensation, the sensation that I'm suspended in time and space. If I happen to be outside, I'll be left standing quite alone. All alone because I can't see a tree, a bush, a hillside, a far ridge, or my own cabin. There's just me and the swirling clouds. And it can bring within its droplets of mist, an extremely disorienting sensation.

However, if I don't allow that disorienting sensation to "cloud" my rationality, I'm also aware that just a few miles away the mountainsides and other valleys are ablaze in the brilliance of a clear sky, awash in warming sunshine. It's this thought–that undeniable solid facet of reality just beyond the cloud–that transforms the eerie aloneness I feel and brings the greater realization that this isolation is only a temporary one. The bright sunrays will soon touch that far ridge, move down and across the valley, and once again illuminate my face with their kiss that soothes my anxious heart and worried soul. And . . . everything quickly returns to normal. My world has righted itself. All is as it should be, and the time has arrived when I can release that long-held sigh of relief.

Those thick blankets of clouds carry a message within their droplets. The Old Woman of the Woods silently points Her gnarled finger at their shrouded mistiness and almost imperceptibly inclines Her head toward them with the intention of inviting us to glean that message. And so, in Her inimitable manner, She softly suggests that there is something of great import we should be perceiving within that roiling grayness–something beyond the surface appearance and the chill it sent over our skin and through our minds. She's kindly pointing to the distinctive signature of Tao. The Tao in whatever form it reveals itself helps us address the most problematical psychological elements in our lives.

Doubts and fears.

The human feeling of disorientation and the sense of aloneness brought on by doubts and fears can be overwhelming and disabling. Yet it doesn't have to be that way if one just understands that many of the doubts and fears that visit us are as insubstantial as that bank of misty cloud passing over. Those doubts and fears don't have to give rise to an all-consuming and prolonged state of negativity or depression once one realizes that the emotionally chilling sensation will pass, leaving the bright sunshine in its silent wake.

Life is rife with all manner of doubts and fears. These shadows can cloud a person's ability to perceive reality for what it is instead of what it *appears* to be, as seen through personal misperceptions and misunderstandings. These doubts and fears skew the reality of Reality in one's life. They darken it with those shifting shadows that, if allowed, consume one's rationality, logic, and confidence.

I'd be incorrect to imply that there are those walking among us who never, ever have experienced some type of doubt or fear that darkened their perspective on life. I strongly believe that no one has escaped these kinds of feelings completely. Good grief, I've had my own share of both, and I'm not ashamed to share a few examples, because some of you may relate to the doubts and fears I've had.

For the most part (probably about 98 percent), the correspondence I've received from my readers worldwide has expressed extremely positive attitudes toward the philosophical content of my books. This support has been a great comfort to me; these letters encourage me to continue writing and give detailed examples of how my words and concepts have helped the letter writers see reality more clearly. More times than I can count, I've heard the sentiment that one of my books saved a reader's life. Never figuring that my literary works would have this kind of impact on others, I was overwhelmed by these letters. To say that they gave me great encouragement to continue writing would be a gross understatement. It was these kind-hearted readers who pulled me through some of my own rough stages in life and, collectively, supported me when my knees felt like they were going to buckle.

So what happened? Why did doubts worm their way into my mind? I foolishly allowed the critical input of that remaining 2 percent of my readership's correspondence to make its way into my consciousness. I admit that it was all due to my own actions. Not being in the habit of discounting the content of my correspondents' letters (all of them), I took them to heart. I took to heart the bad with the good and therefore began to doubt the effectiveness of my spiritual purpose.

Doubt can help us balance our impetuous moves or it can act as an insidiously destructive force in our lives. I hope that, through my own example, others will see the folly of allowing oneself to become entangled and brought down by this unnecessary shadow.

The letters from those 2 percent of my readers were vile and cruel. Instead of looking beyond their words, I took them at face value and internalized them. They pulled dark doubts into my mind–doubts that made me question whether I was wording my books' spiritual concepts precisely enough. What was I to think when so many of my ideas were being so wholely misconstrued? I'd always strived to say things in the most simple manner in order to prevent such misunderstandings, yet it seemed that, somewhere along the line, I didn't quite succeed. Or did I?

When the disorienting cloud passed and warming sunlight shed brightness on the subject, I saw the psychological webs that this small percentage of my readership were weaving to create such hateful letters. It wasn't me at all. It wasn't the manner in which I was presenting the material. Clarity returned to my thinking when I realized that the world is composed of billions of unique individuals, all constructing their thoughts and processing their perceptions in different manners. Each individual passes experiences and information through the sieve of her or his personalized set of attitudes, psychological composition, emotions, prejudices, and belief systems.

Where I went wrong by internalizing the negativity of that 2 percent was that I temporarily forgot you can't please everyone. Yet I wasn't striving to please everyone. My goal was making simplicity and clarity the essence of my writings. It was my doubt about whether I was achieving this goal that confounded me. I realized that the very fact everyone is different means that everyone possesses various levels of intelligence, of reason, of abilities to perceive concepts without interjecting personal attitudes or psychological elements. And so the clouds of doubt I'd experienced regarding this issue dissipated and, forever after, the negative letters had no effect on me.

I hope that many of you will be able to apply the same premise to your own lives. One thoughtless comment or a few negative attitudes expressed by others cannot be allowed to outweigh the goodness you know you have in your heart. Those acts of unkindness cannot be allowed to cloud your sunshine. To internalize the negative and ignore the positive is a choice you freely make. And that choice is what determines whether or not your worldview will be one of shadows or one of sunlight. It determines whether or not you'll live a life darkened by melancholia or depression, or one of childlike delight in your countless blessings. Dark or bright. Sad or happy. Angry or accepting. They all come about as the result of a choice made by each and every person. That choice is each person's right to make. And it's a right everyone should make the most of.

Another prime example drawn from my own experience is the matter of doubting one's worth. This is probably one of the most common doubts folks have. I've certainly read about it time and time again in my correspondent's letters.

When my marriage of twenty-nine years began falling to pieces, I tried many times to gather up the shards and paste them back together. Each time I failed. Whenever I asked my mate what was wrong and how we could fix it, the response I received was the same: "You don't understand, so never mind."

How can you mend what hasn't been identified as broken? Naturally, you try to analyze your life–your relationship–and you wring out your brain like a wet rag in an effort to discover which elements need repair. But this can be a futile effort, because the elements one identifies are generally way off the mark.

With no input from my partner, I began to come up with what I thought the reasons for our problems were. I suspected that my age was one of the major factors. Although I always tried to keep up my appearance for my mate, I couldn't conceal the wrinkles that'd begun to show or the various other physical signs of aging that started visiting me. Once I suspected my age as the problem, I got to work. I vanquished the increasing silver in my hair by applying a permanent dye, and people commented that it took ten years off my looks. Yet nothing I did toward trying to remain attractive seemed to help our situation.

Then I thought that maybe our love life needed improving. I splurged on a large, dark pine canopy bed with mirrors covering the underside of the top. Surely, I thought, that'd spice things up. It didn't. Not a whit.

Then, little by little, my partner began to chip away at my individual rights. Those included the right to receive a phone call, the right to visit friends (or even to *have* a friend). If I wanted to go watch a video at a friend's house in the evening, I was accused of abandonment because I wasn't staying home with my mate. Yet he was gone most of the day with his friends (mostly of the female variety). And it was this last element–the increasing suppression of my rights–that opened my eyes. It wasn't me at all. There was much, much more behind our crumbling relationship. One day I started to stand up for my rights. As a result, my partner went into rages and began wielding guns. I started to fear for my life and sanity and made a quick retreat to my writing cabin for safety.

When I'd tried time and time again to work things out and get my husband some professional help, he refused. When he was the one to voice the dreaded D word–divorce–I adamantly resisted. However, my resistance only exacerbated his resolve, and finally I relented. He got his divorce. And though, for a time, my life felt as though it was torn asunder, someone was there to help me bring those pieces back together, mend my heart, and find love again.

Having doubts about oneself and internalizing the reasons for events involving other people is common to many women. And with all my heart I hope my example will help you see that plunging yourself into that kind of self-doubting behavior is terribly destructive. I agree that it's entirely natural to look first to yourself when faced with a partnership that is souring. You examine your appearance, your behavior, your motives, your *everything*! Yet often it isn't you at all. Many times the *cause* you're so desperately trying to identify is not something that *you've* changed, it is something your *mate* has changed. And when one's mate suddenly develops a completely new set of ideals and goals, there's not a thing you can do about it. If your mate has gone through a metamorphosis like this, you are, in essence, living with a stranger. Sometimes people change. At least consider this possibility when you examine your situation. Don't immediately place all of the blame on yourself. Look at your situation from all sides. Your partner may have changed, you may have changed, or you both may have changed.

My example was like many of those shared with me by others. Although the end result–the divorce–was permanent, the months of being consumed with false doubts about self proved to be a temporary phase . . . just like that bank of clouds that eventually moves on and leaves the comforting and predictable touch of sunshine on your face once again. The familiar points of reference return, and life again has recognizable elements, which are as effective at grounding us as lightning rods are at grounding the potentially damaging electrical charge that hits one's home.

Folks allow all types of doubts to ramble around in their heads, obscuring their ability to recognize their most simple and obvious blessings, and darkening their days with phantom perspectives that encumber their ability to reason. Generally, we don't intentionally set out to do this to ourselves, yet it happens just the same because we possess this wonderfully noble desire to have things right in our lives and in the lives of those around us whom we dearly love and cherish. Healthy people usually shun or try to avoid emotionally disruptive situations, relationships, and events.

One type of doubt that people frequently face is the one associated with their religious belief system. Many torture themselves by vacillating between the strict dogma they're required to accept unconditionally and those exceptions they find continually sprouting from the fertile ground of their minds. These religious doubts can wreak havoc because they generate guilt. If doubt in a belief is present, then the belief doesn't have the necessary strength of conviction to support it. One is caught up in the net of continued belief out of fear of recrimination. This is coerced belief. If one continues the charade of belief who is the loser? The person publicly exhibiting fidelity to an empty belief to appease peers, family, or congregation isn't being true to herself or himself. This kind of masquerade only obscures one's true feelings. Eventually, the stress worsens until one can no longer live with the charade. When that final step is taken to live true, one feels the sun on one's face for the first time in a long while and ultimately feels great relief.

Clouds of doubt come in all shapes and sizes. Some are billowy and white, while others are dark and suffocating. There are doubts that we direct toward ourselves and those we associate with the people around us. We doubt our abilities, our reason, our choices and decisions. Yet by this doubting, we fill our lives with disorienting elements that need not be. We encircle ourselves with confusion and a continual state of turmoil. However, Time appears to be one of the sunrays that dispels those clouds because, eventually, when the doubts are proven to be a temporary phase, everything works out.

Fears.

Now fears represent a far greater force than doubts.

There's a whole category of fears associated with one's perception of self and self-esteem. We already touched upon this issue in the last chapter, yet I'd like to re-emphasize its importance here since so many people struggle with this issue.

The fear of not being liked by others or not considered "as good as another" can result from a sense of inferiority or it can be generated from a narcissistic psychosis. The former is of the more generalized and innocuous type, felt by many; the latter is a serious aberration. The latter type of behavior sifts everything through a sieve of self. The former is more self-demoralizing than self-serving. I'm not even going to address the latter variety, because it's such a serious disorder that it requires a psychiatrist's attention. It's the former type that can often be helped by taking the time to go through a few reasonable considerations about it.

First, I want to be completely forthright by admitting that I myself have a touch of this inferiority thing. Shocked to hear that? I'm terribly shy around people, and that shyness gives them the mistaken impression that I'm being aloof. Nothing could be further from the truth. I'm just not a great conversationalist. I know that many of you struggle with the same shyness in a group setting. This, for me, is a contradictory attitude because I'm comfortable with my own beingness. To be perfectly comfortable with myself and at the same time feel less worth than those around me when in a group of people seems almost silly. Go figure. Well, in the process of that "figuring," I've found that shyness is an inherent characteristic. With the trait of shyness woven through his or her natural beingness, a person can still feel a sense of inadequacy around others–even if that person is really comfortable with the unique beingness of self. So shyness generates qualities that are associated with inferiority.

Here, though, I'm addressing those who feel this sense of inadequacy around others yet are *not* comfortable with their own beingness. These people have all kinds of emotional distress.

As I've said before, we are all individuals. *Individuals.* People who feel inferior to others need to give some serious contemplative thought to that word and all it implies, because I don't believe that most folks understand the full scope of its meaning.

We're all *individuals.* Not one of us is exactly the same as another. We may share some physical likenesses. We may share some interests and philosophies, but those commonalities don't make us *exactly like* another. It's because of our individuality that we're all so wonderfully special. Each person is special. Think about that. Special. *Special* also means unique. Different. One of a kind. You are a one-of-a-kind person. Nobody on this planet (and there are a lot of people walking around on this planet) is just like you. You are the result of a unique mold that produced only one product–you. Everyone came from her or his own separate mold. Even twins are different from each other.

So! How can all these one-of-a-kinds be any more or less valuable than all the others? Uniqueness carries great value. And to fear that special individuality and fear that great value each of us has shows a lack of understanding of the high worth of both.

I've felt bad that some folks have interpreted my quiet nature as evidence of elevated self-worth. That bothers me because it's a judgment based on misperception. Yet I'm who I am, and I understand that I'm unique–just like you are. Just like all of us are. And it's important to remember that that uniqueness is expressed in a variety of ways.

You need to *like* the Who of you. Enjoy the qualities that set you apart from others. Come to the wonderfully freeing realization that not everyone will understand the Who of you. By doing this you'll come to accept other's reactions in a more positive manner. Rather than internalize the negative responses from people, you can let them roll off your well-oiled emotional back by understanding that they're entitled to their uniqueness of attitude and opinion . . . the same as you are. The key is to *cherish* your individuality rather than allow some elements of it to make you cower in public. You are who you are. And conformity doesn't suit you well. It doesn't suit any of us well. Conformity chokes the individuality and all of its beautiful attributes right out of us. The sense of inferiority produces embarrassment, humiliation, fear of recrimination, fear of not being accepted or liked. Yet being true to self is far more noble than conforming to the mold of others.

Fears.

I've written about a wide range of premonitions I've had over the years coupled with the predictive visions of my mentor. Consequently, I've become keenly aware of a growing sense of futility in some people's perspectives. Naturally, I never meant to instill a fear of the future but rather strived to perpetuate a deeper sense of *hope.* Perhaps an even better term than *hope* would be *faith.*

People who fear the future have no sense of the moment. They'll never really be able to cherish each blessed moment gifted them because they're way too busy worrying about their tomorrows instead. Yet no tomorrow is ever reached before today is lived through . . . hour by hour, minute by minute. Those who live for their tomorrows don't live with an awareness of their todays. And, most important, those who live in fear of their tomorrows never truly live the Moment of any of their days. They perceive the passing of time as a negative. They view the passing of time as bringing the specter of death and doom one day closer.

Personally, I don't see the point of living at all if one is going to live in the future. If one's mind is consumed with fears of what that future will be like, one is making one's life a travesty. People who do this do not recognize the beauty of all the blessings that are laid before them each day. Living in fear of the future is the same as having no faith. It's choosing to live constantly in a state of hopelessness where that proverbial glass of water is not only half empty but also polluted water in a filthy glass! Oh, what a depressing way to live. What a crime against self one perpetrates with a fear of the future. To so blatantly ignore the splendorous gifts of the Creatrix alone is a slap in Her sweet face.

Why would folks choose to focus their thoughts on dark

probabilities instead of on the bright ones? That's just what they're doing when they fear the future. Gloom and doom reign. Going around beating one's breast and moaning about depressing possibilities that may never happen seems to be a very self-destructive way to live, especially when there are so many positive elements to reap joy and happiness from. Just think what these people are causing themselves to miss out on.

This type of fear has no redeeming value whatsoever. Fear cannot alter the future. Fear has no power to change probabilities. It carries no benefits. It doesn't contribute to physical or mental health but rather eats away at both like a runaway cancer or an out-of-control brushfire. Fear consumes everything in its path. Worry can do the same. And those who allow either to overtake their lives choose to remain beneath the chilling gray cloud of disorienting reality. When one is clouded with fear and worry, nothing will be perceived with clarity. And, worst of all, individuals who live in such a cloud will never know the power and beauty of having Acceptance fill their hearts and minds with peace. Serenity will never be theirs. They will only have their chosen aloneness as they surround themselves with That Which They Cannot See Through.

It would appear that humankind is addicted to scaring ourselves. It seems as though we as a species have some deep-seated requirement to have something (anything) to be frightened of. This idea is best exemplified by those who fear some type of terminal disease is looming in their future (or currently hidden within their bodies just waiting to explode). Some folks live in horror of contracting cancer, Alzheimer's disease, or any number of potentially lethal diseases while their physical health is perfect.

Having this type of fear is like being afraid of the future. It's an insidious attitude to force on yourself because it invites constant negativity that can overshadow the whole of one's days. It's like fearing the sky is going to fall on you at any moment instead of gazing up into that beautiful blue and letting wonderment fill your being with joy and gladness.

Fears with no basis are fears that people *create* a basis for. This is an extremely important statement. *Fears with no basis are fears that people create a basis for.* What does this mean? It underscores the fact that *thoughts are things.* Thoughts are energy applied to a specific life aspect. Therefore, healthy people who continually fear that they will contract a certain illness or disease give thought energy to that illness or disease. It's like they are calling what they fear most to visit them. They are inviting it in with the strong energies of their fearful thoughts.

Leave well enough alone. Count your health as a blessing–a great blessing–and take joy in that gift you've been given. Why ignore that gift by fearing some illness that may never touch your life–even if you live to be a hundred and one years old? Take joy in your health, don't steep yourself in the fear of it being anything less at some point in time.

This concept of thoughts contributing strong energy to an obsessive idea isn't myth or some New Age legend. It's fact. Thoughts are powerful, powerful things. And choosing fear as the subject of those thoughts is as reckless and dangerous as fooling around with a book of matches or toying with a gun.

There's another important aspect of this issue. I'm talking about those individuals already diagnosed with a serious illness or terminal disease. I've witnessed the behavior of some of these folks. Some are in denial. Others fully recognize their disease and accept it with grace. These latter folks are the ones who go on with their lives as normally as they can manage. I take my sunhat off to them because they exhibit great courage in the face of a very negative situation. They continue to recognize each brightening daybreak as the beginning of the *rest* of their lives and give no thought to how many daybreaks they have left. These ill people gaze about their world and become grounded in reality. They do this by understanding their true blessings and focusing their attention on the little joys in life. I greatly admire and deeply respect these people.

But then there are those who, upon being diagnosed with a disease, make that disease their whole world. They constantly talk about it. They can't seem to think about anything else. I'd like to scream at these people. I'd like to grab their shoulders and shake them. I'd like to tell them exactly what they're doing to themselves. They're exacerbating their disease or illness by continually giving energy to it. They can't see reality for the disease. They refuse to see the sunlight for the shadows their disease casts upon their path. They voluntarily refuse to see that proverbial glass as being half full . . . unless, of course, it's half full of their disease. These folks choose to let the disease gut every beautiful element of their lives.

Denial, grace, and total absorption. I've observed all three of these ways people handle their diseases and haven't given much thought to how I'd react if I contracted a serious illness. I don't deny that the discovery would be an initial shock. Nobody wants to have a disease, especially a terminal one. Yet I know in my heart that I wouldn't fear it. I know that I wouldn't ever talk about it to others. I know that I'd choose to focus on the more positive elements of my life because to focus only on the disease and surround myself with its chilling gray cloud would only obscure the chance to reap some measure of joy and happiness from the beauty that friends, loved ones, family, and nature could be gifting me with. I would not choose denial, only acceptance. I'd choose to acknowledge the disease while never giving it mental energy. Instead, my mental energies would be directed at appreciating the good and pleasing aspects my life contained. That philosophy may sound a bit idealistic, but think about it. To do otherwise is a waste of one's energy. To do otherwise is a waste of one's remaining time on earth. It's a choice. It's always a choice. Perspective is a choice. It's a choice to remain isolated in the chilling cloud of disorienting reality or to accept that cloud and allow it to pass so that your face is again bathed in the warmth of your many blessings.

Fear.

This chapter wouldn't be complete without addressing the fear of dying, because some people live their entire lives fearing their end. Granted, everyone walking on this planet has probably, at one time or another, given more than a passing thought to his or her death. We wonder how it'll ultimately happen. Will we feel pain or will it be instantaneous? Violent or peaceful? Wouldn't it be nice if we'd all just make that final transition by going in our sleep? That way there'd be no fear or emotional trauma associated with death. No pain, no last thoughts or regrets. Just a peaceful passing into the new life Beyond.

Yet what quality of life is experienced by those who continually fear their own death? If death is the central focus of one's thoughts, how can one's life be productive, creative, or meaningful? A person living in constant fear certainly can't recognize or appreciate nature's incredible beauty. People with a fearful mind-set definitely don't reap the emotional rewards of receiving the many acts of unconditional goodness others perform for them. The specter of death is their constant companion because that's who they choose to pal around with. All their days are days of darkness as the gunmetal clouds billow higher and higher into towering thunderheads, obscuring all sunlight and warmth in their lives.

A life cannot be emotionally fulfilling if one chooses to take death as one's partner. Life is not what beats us down, our *choice* of *perception* is. It's our attitudes and perspectives, our logic and reason that determine what kind of life we end up living. The sunshine and the temporary banks of clouds that roll in to obscure that light are both natural elements of nature and our lives. How we perceive each is an individual choice.

And so, in Her great wisdom, the gentle Old Woman of the Woods silently points to the banks of clouds that sometimes shroud the mountains and valleys and invites us to recognize the obvious comparisons between the nature of Nature and the nature of humans. She is not judgmental. She does not chastise us for our frequent lack of awareness and our ignorance. She simply generously gifts us with an abundance of natural examples to learn from. She does not force us to take notice. She's content within Her own beingness and, through Her example, wishes with all Her heart that we would reap the endless rewards of intellectually sampling Her bountiful offerings and emotionally savoring their life benefits. In Her world all is natural. All follows the simple cycle of life. All has its unique season upon that curving trail, each a temporary phase of beautiful and diversified individuality. Each carrying the assurance of predictability . . . the predictability of tomorrow's sunrise.

rainbows in a drop of dew—second sight

A SUNBEAM GLINTING OFF A SINGLE DROP OF dew can catch one's attention and, like a magnet, draw the unsuspecting mind to its unspoken call.

Daybreak, casting multiple columns of golden light upon a mountain meadow covered in a profusion of brilliant wildflowers, has the power to capture the heart in a swoon of rapture.

Moondrops of shimmer, reflecting their wildly erotic dance upon the laughing waters of a singing stream, dazzle the soul and encourage it to participate in the feral celebration of life.

"What nonsense!" Is that what you thought about what you just read? Did you think the statements were nothing more than some fanciful ramblings tumbling from a very imaginative author's head? Did you think they were figments out of a child's mystical fairy tale? Just so much background atmosphere for the telling of an old magical legend? Perhaps the stuff science fiction is made of?

Ahh, then good, you're just the kinds of folks this chapter is written for. So settle down in your chair for a magical ride right into the center of a drop of dew.

If you think my statements about the sunbeam, the daybreak, and the moondrops are just so much literary fluff thrown down for the purpose of stuffing the pages of a book, you're wrong–dead wrong. At least maybe you thought they were simply a string of adjectives used to gussy up the commonness of nature. Huh? Well, the truth is, the whole point of this chapter is that I don't have any *need* to gussy up nature's attributes. Nobody does. In fact, for a writer to make such an attempt would border on the sacrilegious, since nature in and of itself possesses far more inherent magnificence than any human being could dream of conjuring up for it. Why, to my way of thinking, it would be the height of human arrogance to think anyone could improve on nature. Don't you think so too? Rather than feeling arrogance toward nature, I always become humbled in its presence. It is so awesome!

Awesome! There's no other word existing or devised (in any language) that comes within a mile of accurately describing the glorious splendor of nature. Not one! And when you think of the wonderful array of terms that are synonymous with *beauty,* it is damn amazing. It's pretty funny to see friends of mine grinning and shaking their heads when hearing my descriptive word creations associated with nature.

Beautimous.

Gorgymous!

Oh, I know, you don't have to tell me how ridiculous those

nonwords sound. And I'd be the first to agree that they're nothing but silly, nonsensical words that sound more like a small child's attempt to utter the right word. Yet in my exuberance these word creations just seem to spill out of my mouth when I'm overcome by the high excitement and joy that nature fills my heart with.

However, words are just words, after all. Therefore, some words aren't composed of letters at all. Some words aren't conveyed by the spoken voice, nor are they read on a sheet of paper. Some words aren't transmitted by either of these forms of communication because they *can't* be. Some words (the precise words) can be conveyed only as a *feeling*. But . . . only if you first have the eyes to see them. Only if your ears are attuned to them. Only if your heart is opened to them and your soul receptive to their powerfully moving impact. Uh-huh, that's what this chapter is all about. Awareness–our psyche's beautiful and unequaled, innate quality of Second Sight.

Second Sight.

Perhaps you thought this section was going to be on psychic abilities. Wrong. This section isn't about premonitions, crystal gazing, how to read someone's mind, or how to communicate with ghosts. It's solely about the type of Second Sight few folks even recognize as Second Sight, much less show any interest in expending effort on developing–your common, everyday garden variety of mental and emotional Awareness. Sometimes it's referred to by its other name, Sensitivity. *Perceptual* sensitivity, to be more precise.

Perceptual sensitivity. Okay, what makes that so important to write about? And, more to the point, why's it so critical to a book on what the Old Woman of the Woods has to convey to us about what nature can teach? What's it got to do with the Tao of Nature?

Let's begin by going back to that dewdrop–back to that

rainbow in a drop of dew idea, because that's where the answers to these questions can be found.

A world of surface images is on display to the naked eye. With mere surface awareness, everything is seen on an exterior level because that's the perception used to view it. Nothing deeper. No depth of perception exists, so there is no depth of *realization* that there's anything *more* to see or discover. Yet with the advent of the microscope, binoculars, and even more powerful tools, such as the CAT scan, MRI, X ray, and sonogram, we've found that what is seen with the naked eye is, indeed, only surface reality and that there's much more beyond and within that surface presentation.

However, people don't need any of these tools to broaden their worldview when they have a perceptual awareness that goes far beyond the surface characteristics of the many elements in their world. This ability of Second Sight is a natural skill that everyone possesses. You don't need to be a psychic or mystic to see what is beyond the obvious in life. All you have to do is have an awareness (an understanding) that everything is always so much more than it initially appears to be.

A dewdrop is a dewdrop is a dewdrop until . . . one gets down on hands and knees and really *looks* at it. Not only does it have sparkle but it has substance. It has a surface that glistens and reflects everything around it. It's like a mirror, and you can see your own image within it. Not only your image but the images of everything around you. That tiny drop of dew is much like those large garden globes that capture the presence of everything around them. A drop of dew is so full of color–it's as if a magical rainbow has been caught within its essence. That little drop of water holds a universe of images, each separate from the other yet all contained within a single bit of moisture poised on a velvety flower petal.

So beautiful.

So fragile.

Yet so amazingly full of images rarely seen.

Images that fill the human mind with wonder, but only if they are perceived with eyes that see the revelations Second Sight brings to the human heart and soul.

Epiphanies.

Solutions to problems.

Deep insights.

Serenity. The serenity that's the tranquil by-product of growing wisdom.

Now we've reached the point in the chapter where all those wonderful-sounding adjectives have a hands-on application.

Perceptual awareness involves all aspects of one's life. It's not just the reading of someone's body language for the purpose of gleaning additional insights into his or her hidden character or intentions. It's also taking notice of someone's specific choice of words, being aware of response times when a question or favor is asked. These are subtle yet telling indicators of how someone's thinking. They're leads into the inner self that the perceptive individual can follow.

Conversational characteristics aren't the only markers connected to personality, there's also mode of dress. We touched on this in "Glittering Gold–Understanding Value," but in that context the subject was associated with individuality. And dress does show whether a person is a conformist or feels comfortable enough with the beingness of self to be unconventional or even eccentric. So outward appearances, like conversational qualities, are clear perceptual clues that the aware individual can pick up on and add to the total picture of another person.

People, all people, are enigmas. They're enigmas because they're all separate entities with different personalities, attitudes, behavioral responses, opinions, philosophies, beliefs, agendas, and so on. Everyone is an enigma . . . on the outside. Just like that dewdrop is just a dewdrop until one makes the concerted effort to take that closer look. Even that seemingly visible conformist who is afraid to express individuality and dresses like his or her peers and behaves the same way is an enigma. Even though that individual may make every effort to conform, all elements of himself or herself are only external trappings, which conceal the real self hidden within. This is what the perceptually aware person understands and sees. This is what Second Sight allows one to perceive with ease. In fact, I saved this chapter for last because, in reality, this entire book is about second sight, as the Old Woman of the Woods so adeptly teaches us with Her many facets of nature.

Our physical eyes spy a particularly beautiful sunset, yet without bothering to engage our innate ability of perceptual awareness, we remain unmoved by that magnificent sight. We end up seeing only the surface visual without reaping the emotional rewards it was meant to gift us with. Not recognizing that there is so much more worth and value associated with nearly everything we see, we're behaving in a no more human manner than robots mechanically walking through life. We are never experiencing the soft and soothing undercurrents that have the potential to instill in us serenity and deeper wisdom.

How many times have you driven to work and, once there, had the thought that you didn't see or remember one thing about your trip? That's a sign of mental preoccupation. That's just one simple example of not staying focused. That's not only perceptual unawareness, that's complete unawareness. And I can't say I've never done that, either. We all have. Yet just because we all do it doesn't mean it's okay. We need to stay focused on whatever we're doing if we expect to be aware individuals. Accidents happen because we allow our awareness to slip away. Cruel statements are voiced because our perceptual awareness gets lost in the emotion of the moment. And then, if we're decent folk, we feel regret and guilt because our mouths followed some knee-jerk emotion instead of reflecting some of the intellect and the wisdom we pride ourselves in having. *There is no wisdom without perceptual awareness and its attendant sensitivity.* The intellect can have smarts, but without perceptual awareness and sensitivity that intellect is bereft of wisdom. Multitudes of highly intelligent people come and go through this world of ours. I've been in the presence of a few of them. However, even fewer gave any evidence of true wisdom generated by perceptual awareness and *spiritual* sensitivity.

We make our journey through life over pathways, roads, highways, and superhighways. Some of these are straight, and others have convoluted turns and hairpin curves. Some roads are well worn by the footfalls of those who have passed ahead of us; other trails we blaze ourselves. Yet no matter which path is taken, we ultimately miss all there is to learn along the way if we never take our shoes off. Those shoes are the blinders with which we voluntarily cover our Second Sight. Those shoes act as insulation against sensitivity and clear perception. If we travel in such a state, that drop of dew is seen as nothing more than a piece of moisture. Sometimes it's never noticed at all.

We live in such an awesome world. There is so much to be wonder-struck over, so much created with the dynamic power to soothe the stressed and harried mind. So many beautiful facets of nature that sparkle their splendor in an effort to get our attention and invite us to partake emotionally of their gifts of wisdom.

How can we choose to ignore all these blessings, seeing only what's on the surface of life? How can we not take every opportunity to be as perceptively sensitive to our world as possible? Happiness and serenity are not illusions. They're not an ancient legend or myth. They're real. They're very real. They're real and easily accessible to each and every one of us. All we need to do is to reach out and *touch*.

Reach. Reach out with our awareness and perceive.

Touch. Touch with our sensitivity–our emotional sensitivity.

And see. And finally . . . see. See the magnificent reality *beneath* the surface reality we once called real.

Second Sight. It's not a skill gifted to a few genuine psychics. It's an *innate* quality of perception granted to *every* human being as a most valuable divine inheritance. It's yours to claim. It's a sacred gift offered to each one of us.

By participating in a little private quiz you can get a sense of whether you're viewing life with perceptual sensitivity and seeing beyond the surface skin of reality.

When you see a baby, do you see it as a wonderful miracle of life?

If you witness a toddler throwing a fit in a store, do you see that child's potential as a productive adult?

When those bright yellow dandelions sprout in your lawn, do you ever get down on hands and knees and appreciate how pretty the fluffy blossoms are? Or make use of the leaves as salad greens high in vitamin C?

If you've ever driven down a country road and come upon a recent roadkill, have you pulled it off the road out of respect for its former life force?

Have you ever stopped to think about all the benefits a tree contributes to the overall environment of the planet (and humankind)?

What philosophical concept does a minnow convey?

When nature goes dormant over winter, do you tend to think of it as a dead time or as a resting phase of its cycle?

In your opinion, is an eccentric a weird person?

Which holds more promise, a sunrise or a sunset?

Does an outgoing extrovert reveal more about character and personality than a quiet introvert?

Is a weed or a fine grass more desirable?

What *personal* qualities make a film star so popular in the public's eye?

Is peer opinion important to you?

Which individual carries more power, the president of a country or the citizen?

How important is your nationality to you? Or the ethnicity of another?

What philosophical message is conveyed by a thunderstorm?

Do you believe in fairies? Why or why not?

What can you tell from someone's tone of voice?

Do you have to see or touch something in order to believe in it?

What's your initial reaction upon seeing a homeless person?

Would you quit your high-paying job as an objection to the unfair firing of a co-worker or blatant illegal practices of your company?

What redeeming qualities does a thistle have?

If you live in the city, how do you view pigeons?

What does a badger have to teach us?

Does being lost have any positive aspects associated with it?

How does having a hypochondriac friend or family member give us valuable insights into human behavior?

When you notice a swallow circling its nest, does that behavior inspire philosophical insights or pieces of wisdom?

What's more revealing regarding a person's true attitude, words or behavior?

Can you recognize the difference between the opinions of others based on fact and those colored by attitude or emotion, such as jealousy, revenge, hatred, prejudice, and the like?

Whose expressed appreciation of you carries more worth, your boss's or your child's?

How can you tell the difference between a crow and a raven?

What does seeing a rainbow mean to you? A falling star?

Can a fly teach us anything about human behavior?

Have you ever given thought to a butterfly's life cycle?

When a friend gets angry with you, what's your immediate response?

Ants. What philosophical concepts can they convey to us? What jewels of wisdom can we glean from watching their behavior?

What can an earthworm teach us?

Have you taken note of anything special about the time of twilight?

Are all illnesses karmically induced?

Does day carry more clarity than night?

Does the full moon illumine more than the new moon?

Who represents more honesty and integrity, a minister or a business associate?

What does one's continual refusal to volunteer for something really mean?

What does spying an elk, deer, or mountain goat bring to mind?

If you are confronted by a panhandler, what's your initial thought?

Which has the potential to impart philosophical concepts, a bat or a rabbit?

Does a moonbeam teach us more than a sunray?

Which is more pleasing to your eye, a carefully tended

English garden or a field of wildflowers? Which one has the greater philosophical concepts to convey with respect to gaining insights into attained wisdom?

When you're out in public, do you take note of who's around you?

These questions are but a few that, when answered honestly, will give you some insight into your level of perceptual awareness. Second Sight is seeing beyond, beneath, above, around, and through everything you see with the naked eye. It's like putting everything you see on a computer screen and rotating the visual so that you can clearly see it from all angles. Yet it's even more than that because when you use your Second Sight you're perceiving multidimensionally . . . with the soul.

afterword

I SINCERELY BELIEVE THAT EVERY SINGLE ONE OF us, from the teenager to the elder, from the nurse to the casino blackjack dealer or the CEO, wants to feel more grounded in our lives. None of us–not a one–enjoys constant stress, frustration, or a harried existence in which there's never any room for serenity or peace. So happiness is what we desire most. We're not asking for the world here, we're not asking for a life of never-ending happiness, we're just wanting to have a little more pleasure so that our lives can be more balanced. We quest for greater measures of happiness and joy to fill our hearts so that life's darker nights are lit by more full moons and starshine. Consequently, many of us look far and wide, hoping to spy the glorious object of our quest.

Elusiveness can be a stubborn quality of happiness for those who don't know its face. Some folks think happiness lies in the possession of stuff; they drive themselves frantic collecting and collecting yet still are left unfulfilled and wondering why they're not satisfied. Others believe happiness is having power, so they lead controlling and manipulative lives that ultimately leave them alone with cold power as their only companion or friend. Some people are convinced that owning a big house will bring them the most happiness, yet upon obtaining that long-desired property they find there's still some inexplicable yearning left in their hearts. And then there are those who believe that surrounding themselves with a large circle of friends will bring them all the happiness they'd ever want, only to discover that they'd forgotten to factor in the reality that friends eventually move away and few relationships last forever.

Happiness is so often sought in all the wrong places and for all the wrong reasons. That's why the quest for it is so longstanding. The Old Woman of the Woods knows this well, for She is as wise as Her ancient yet seemingly ageless years. She has never stopped attempting to get our attention, to help us questing and wandering humans to notice the Tao of Nature and the great heights of happiness, joy, and deep wisdom we can reap from it without even having to search. It's right there under our noses. It's right there in front of our eyes. Always has been. Second Sight brings it into crisp focus. Perceptual awareness brings it into our hearts, minds, and souls. All we have to do is open up our eyes, ears, and hearts to experience the awesome sensations we're filled with when we allow nature to gently envelope the totality of our beingness–when we abandon our hard shields of resistance and pull off our blinders to . . . bring it home.

As surely as you and I breathe, nature also inhales and

exhales. And whispers of high wisdom can be heard on the breath of each wafting breeze. Sweet whispers are heard from the tender heart of the Old Woman of the Woods as She quietly calls to each one of us. What wonders to behold! What epiphanies of wisdom! What pure enchantment!

If only we'd listen.

index